BELFAST TAXI

A drive through history, one fare at a time

LEE HENRY

BLACKSTAFF PRESS
BELFAST

First published in 2012 by
Blackstaff Press
4c Heron Wharf
Sydenham Business Park
Belfast BT3 9LE
with the assistance of
The Arts Council of Northern Ireland

arts
council
of Northern Ireland

Typeset by CJWT Solutions, St Helens, England

Printed in Berwick-upon-Tweed by Martins the Printers

A CIP catalogue record for this book
is available from the British Library

ISBN 978-0-85640-888-5

www.blackstaffpress.com

www.blackstaffpress.com/ebooks

To all those drivers who lost their lives
during the Troubles,
and to my parents, Fiona and Jim

Contents

Introduction

Belfast Taxi: A drive through history, one fare at a time is an oral history of the taxi industry in Northern Ireland's capital city told through interviews with drivers of all ages and from various backgrounds – Catholic and Protestant, male and female, young and old, Northern Irish and from further afield. It explores the working lives and memories of Belfast's many and varied taxi drivers: to find out what drew them to the profession in the first place, what pressures and pleasures they derive from their jobs and, ultimately, what keeps them clocking in.

I am, of course, not the first person to take an interest in Belfast taxis and their drivers. Both have been the subject of many works, including Brendan Ellis's 1989 series of drawings, *A Year in the Black Taxis,* and Laurence McKeown's 2009 play, *Two Roads West.*

My fascination was sparked close to home. My adoptive grandfather, Cecil Henry, worked in Belfast as a public-hire taxi driver. He died when I was four, and I have few memories of him, but I do have an old black and white photograph. In it my grandfather, dressed smartly in a double-breasted jacket and polished shoes, poses beside his very own black hackney cab on a residential street in east Belfast. It is a fascinating image – it shows that in 1940s Belfast, taxi driving was a vocation to be proud of.

Later, when I moved to Belfast from the seaside town of Newcastle in 2005, I would call for a taxi every morning to take me into town: a journey of around one mile. During those journeys I met many drivers, and got to know some quite well. Their banter and conversation helped me come to terms with the world each morning. I learned about their loves, lives and losses, their passions, pastimes and pet hates. Gerry loved classical music and prided himself on introducing the drunken hordes to Tchaikovsky, rather than Tiësto, on a Saturday night. Billy Scott had a degree in sociology and was Northern Ireland's first registered taxi tour-guide. Tom was shot through the shoulder during an attempted carjacking in the 1980s. And Fionola, the only female driver in her depot, was champion arm wrestler for the third year running – 'no word of a lie'.

The drivers' stories came thick and fast and, as a journalist, I was more than happy to hear them. If I didn't happen to agree with some of their views on religion, politics or sport, they never rammed them down my throat. Once, when I suggested to one driver that Manchester United would surely surpass Liverpool in the trophy stakes (I'm pleased to say I was right!), he smiled, winked and said: 'You might be a journalist, but at least you've got a sense of humour.'

Of course, it's difficult to be objective about taxi drivers. We all have our own opinions of them. Ask some residents in Belfast what they think of local taxi drivers and you will get plenty of unflattering adjectives to take home and ponder. Shifty, coarse, vocal. Greedy, negligent, abrasive. However, I know from experience that this isn't the whole story. Belfast taxi drivers are opinionated, personable and forthright, and in that way, are no different to their international counterparts in cities around the world, but their experiences of working in the Troubles set them apart.

I was told of instances when drivers had been forced to dive for cover during bombings and shootings as their press corps passengers jostled for position; of hijackings; of drivers who had had their taxis sequestered by paramilitaries and used to transport arms or explosive devices into town. They told me of their colleagues, men they had worked with for years, who were murdered by paramilitaries for no other reason than the fact they were either Catholic or Protestant. Their stories were often horrifying – but instilled in me a sincere sense of respect and admiration, and a willingness to play a part in recording this part of Belfast's history.'

Belfast is unique in that it has three different types of taxi: public-hire taxi-buses and private- and public-hire taxi cars. Passengers book private-hire cabs, or minicabs, over the phone or online, while public-hire cabs – the black hackney cabs that are especially synonymous with London – are available to anyone who waves them down, or who queues at a designated public-hire rank. Although public-hire taxis in Belfast are informally known as 'black hacks', they are not always black – they come in a variety of colours, and some act as mobile advertising hoardings.

The public-hire taxi-buses are operated by the West Belfast Taxi Association (WBTA) and the Shankill Taxi Association (STA), and are unique to Belfast. Again, these are standard black hackney cabs, but they operate along designated routes in and out of the west and north of the city. They are really like buses, transporting up to eight people at a time on a first come, first serve basis – with passengers even sitting in the front of the taxi with the driver – and filling up with whoever is waiting at the stand, so the fare per person is much cheaper than a standard taxi fare. This type of taxi came into operation in the early 1970s when bus services to the most troubled areas of Belfast were often suspended.

★

It was clear that the majority of drivers I spoke to wanted their stories to be heard – something they thought was long overdue – and they encouraged me to go ahead with this book. So I began to arrange some interviews, and found the response encouraging, if perhaps a little slow at the beginning. Very few of the drivers I approached refused outright to speak to me and those that did – after overhearing their fellow drivers waxing lyrical about the nature of foreign investment in the city or the ongoing public/private-hire war – would often speak at length about a subject without any hesitation when asked again for their opinion. Indeed, it was frequently the hesitant ones who turned out to be the most informative and eloquent.

Sometimes it was not an easy task to get the interviewees to open up when the tape was rolling. When they're in their cabs and comfortable with their lot, Belfast taxi drivers can talk for Ulster. But bring a microphone into the equation and things can get decidedly quiet, decidedly quick. Suffice it to say that I spent more money on cigarettes, bottles of beer and cups of tea during the interview process than I ever would have imagined possible, and smoked and drank a few too many myself.

Many drivers preferred not to talk about their upbringings or reveal their religious affiliations, and thus their perceived political allegiances, which is understandable in a city with a history a troubled as Belfast's. Such drivers remained guarded at all times, but I have a fair idea which side of the divide most of the drivers interviewed came from, and know that both communities are represented pretty much equally in this book. Those drivers who were happy for their identities to be known are given their full names in the text. Those who preferred anonymity are referred to by a false first name only.

The vast majority of subjects interviewed were middle-aged men from Belfast. In such a male-dominated industry, it was difficult to find female drivers who had worked in the industry for any length of time, but I did find some and their stories add greatly to the book.

I also interviewed several foreign nationals who had moved to Northern Ireland some years ago and who had worked as cabbies for a substantial period, to get their perspectives on Belfast and her inhabitants and to find out if the job is more challenging or, conversely, more enjoyable for the outsider moving in.

I was continually impressed by all the drivers' ability to recall even the smallest pieces of information – from the names of past colleagues, to dates, times and even street names. Most drivers are natural storytellers, though it's worth bearing in mind the following nugget of advice from David McCracken, a former taxi driver for Enterprise Taxis. 'There are plenty of stories to go around,' David told me, his brows raised for emphasis. He leaned in closer and joked, 'but taxi drivers, you must remember, never let the truth get in the way of a good story.'

The taxi drivers are at the heart of this book and in it they tell their stories in their own words. They operate in all areas of Belfast. They know the city intimately: its ever-changing landscape, its shifting, chequered history, its many and varied inhabitants and their many faults and foibles. They know many of them by name. Belfast's taxi drivers keep a close eye on the city and its people because it is in their interests to do so. History happens in their rear-view mirrors, and they rarely forget anything worth retelling. This is their history of Belfast.

The Origins of the Belfast Taxi Trade

> Those who chose to swim against the current,
> those who did the wheeling and dealing and
> made their own way, were the ones who did
> the taxiing.
>
> JOE GRAHAM
> *founder of ACE Taxis and Ardoyne Taxis*

'If you're going to talk about the carrying of people for wages
or earnings you have to mention that it all started with the
sedan-chair carriers,' ex-driver Joe Graham insisted as we
sat for his interview in a room stacked with VCR tapes, self-
published pamphlets, piles of dusty documents and dog-eared
books (many pilfered from libraries across the city), all relating
to the history of Belfast.

Joe, as it turned out, was not only a former taxi driver
and owner of ACE Taxis and Ardoyne Taxis, both founded
in the 1970s, he was also an enthusiastic amateur historian,
author, and editor of the self-published *Rushlight* magazine
and website. He had invited me to his home to examine the
impressive archive he had accumulated over the years, and to
learn about the peculiar intricacies of early taxiing in Belfast.

He explained that in the early-nineteenth century a popular

1

method of transport would have been sedan chairs – wooden cabins, or litters, which were hung from two poles and carried by two strong-armed porters. They were suitable for a single passenger only, and were the preferred method of transport for ladies of leisure, who hired these carriers to take them around town to avoid having their skirts muddied on the dirty streets. This was really the first bona fide form of public-hire vehicle available to the citizens of Belfast, and there would have been a small army of authorised sedan-chair carriers – or 'chair-men' – plying for hire in the city centre.

'The first official sedan-chair stand was located at the corner of Donegall Place and Castle Street,' Joe told me, 'and by law, public sedan carriers had to make an agreed price with their customer to bring them from A to B.' However, this law left something of a loophole, which allowed 'unofficial' chair men to gain a foothold in the trade. 'It meant that if you did not agree a price with your customer, then you weren't in that business. You were a freelancer, in other words.'

The majority of these freelancers would have been working-class Catholics who owned and hired out their own modest sedans, servicing an affluent clientele of Protestant settlers. It was a form of employment that gained particular popularity in the working-class Markets area of the city.

'The Markets was a unique area,' Joe explained. 'Other areas of Belfast grew up around the mills. Workers came in on a promise. They were going to get a two-up, two-down wee house and a regular pay packet on a Friday night and that was it. They stuck to that and moved on. But the Markets people, mostly County Down people, for some reason or other had a singular ability, imagination, flair for initiative, independence, and they went into creating their own livelihoods … They weren't under the control of any linen barons or anything like that and it's important to see that. Those who chose to swim against the current, those who did the wheeling and dealing and made their own way, were the ones who did the taxiing.'

In this way, Joe compares sedan-chair carriers with those

drivers who worked for the West Belfast Taxi Association during the 1970s and 80s. 'Sedan-chair carriers would have been like the black taxis of the Falls Road,' he surmised. 'Although the black hacks are now official – they're numbered and legal and all the rest of it – for years they operated without licences and the authorities turned a blind eye because they were expedient. It was the same for sedan-chair carriers – the authorities turned a blind eye.'

Joe went on to draw further parallels with modern-day taxiing as he related the story of Lord Arthur Chichester and an incident with a sedan chair during a journey through Belfast's city centre in 1836.

'Lord Chichester was going through what we now call Castle Court at Castle Junction, when a bit of a riot broke out,' Joe explained. 'He was scooped out of his sedan and the thing was pulled apart. Now, when I read the official account of it I immediately pictured it in a modern set up. You know, a vehicle and somebody dragged out of it and the car turned over and burned or whatever. It's like nothing changes in history. But it was a sedan, not a black taxi. Two guys carrying it. They'd have been uniformed and all that. They'd have had their crest on the door and probably powdered wigs and three-cornered hats. That was a taxi. That was the first hijacking of a taxi in Belfast!'

Of course, this ornate sedan chair may in fact have been the property of Lord Chichester himself, or his esteemed friend Sir James Emerson Tennent, his companion on the day, as they were both well-to-do and could afford to buy their own chairs and employ their own carriers. Equally possible – or probable, as Joe argues – is that they may have been travelling in sedans for hire.

Public-hire sedan chairs were commonly available in Belfast until the 1840s when sedans went out of fashion for good, but they were not the only 'taxis' in business in the early part of the eighteenth century. *The Town Book of the Corporation of Belfast, 1613–1816* carries a record of regulations, published on 8 May 1701, pertaining to the Corporation of Car-men, a group of thirty licensed commercial drivers who would lease their services, and thus their horses-and-carts, to 'merchants as well as strangers' by transporting goods like salt, coal, wine and butter from ships docked at the wharf to merchants and markets in town. However, they were also required to use their vehicles to transport passengers – namely members of the army and other subjects of the King – if ordered to do so by the town constables.

And, like the sedan-carriers, it seems the car-men also had to contend with unlicensed competitors – identified in the *Belfast Town Book* as 'straglers [sic]' – plying for hire. Lower-class townsfolk in Belfast lucky enough to own, rent or borrow a means of transportation would have made something of a living outside of the law from hiring their services to strangers and townsmen who had produce or people to move.

With cargo ships arriving from Europe and the Americas, unlicensed car-men, keen to profit from Belfast's rise to power, helped to transport foreign sailors into town. Lawmen too, not wanting to muddy their shoes, made solid use of Belfast's illegal car-men until one too many were over-charged, offended by bad driving or struck by a drunken car-man's carriage. Car-men were deemed too unruly, too lawless, perhaps even too self-sufficient to be allowed to continue to operate without further restrictions.

So in Section 338 of the Belfast Improvement Act of 1806, further laws and by-laws governing the practice were subsequently set-down: all public service vehicles used to transport passengers in Belfast were now only permitted to do so after passing several mechanical tests; drinking at the wheel – or at the reins, as the case may have been – was forbidden; not more than the given number of passengers were permitted on board any public-service vehicle; and the name and address of the vehicle's owner was to be printed clearly and precisely on the side of all cabs. Furthermore, unlike today (when public-hire cab drivers are permitted to pick up fares at their own discretion) cab drivers then were legally obliged to stop for whoever happened to wave them down – no matter how inebriated or unattractive the prospective fare appeared to be.

Under the 1806 act, car-men were also now obliged by law to maintain their carriages and horses, making sure that their vehicles were 'well and sufficiently built, hung upon springs, and level', and their horses 'able and sufficient for the work, and free from any infectious disease'. A full-time inspector of carriages ensured that standards were met, wielding the power to make or break any car-man's licence application.

As Belfast steadily grew – with new streets added year by year and the population of the city increasing – the demand for comfortable, secluded, speedy and reliable public-hire vehicles inevitably increased. Well-heeled patrons not wealthy enough to own their own carriages – and thus employ their own coachmen – would hire taxis to take them to Belfast's Grand Opera House for an evening's entertainment or to the Botanic Gardens to see the exotic flora and fauna on display, while men of trade and visiting sailors relied heavily on the multi-passenger, horse-drawn cabs to ferry them into town and out into the surrounding areas.

A watercolour painting by Marcus Ward, commissioned by the owners of the department store Robinson & Cleaver in 1889, provides an invaluable glimpse into the working lives of Belfast's first cabbies. From this painting we can ascertain the different types of cab available for hire in Belfast before the advent of motorised taxis.

The painting is set in Donegall Place, looking down what is now Royal Avenue (formerly Hercules Street) and shows a variety of horse-drawn vehicles available for hire: two-wheel hansom cabs, the pick of the bunch, which provided an enclosed space for passengers; jaunting cars, a two or four-wheel vehicle, with the driver positioned to the side, also used to transport produce; four-wheel landaus, a popular, four-seater carriage with a retractable hood that afforded passengers the opportunity to face one another as they travelled; sociables, fair-weather vehicles with a partial hood like a pram and two drivers; phaetons, leisurely vehicles often with no hood and drawn by a single horse; and Clarence cabs, four-wheeled, enclosed carriages which earned the nickname 'growlers' due to the noise they made when driven over the cobbled streets. These growlers were the Belfast cabs most readily available for hire at the time, but they garnered a poor reputation since they were mainly second-hand and, as a result, frequently ill-equipped or in poor working condition.

If cab owners owned their own horses they would pay a livery-stable owner, such as Christopher Campbell of Ann Street (registered in the 1806 Belfast Street Directory), a weekly or monthly fee to house and feed their horses. Car-men would collect their horses in the morning and replace them at night, at a given hour, before heading home to their families. Horse-drawn taxiing was, according to Joe Graham, a particularly well-paid pursuit. 'During the aul' horse and cart days there were dozens of stables in the Markets ... men with three or four horses and carriages. Some guy would have got a hold of one of the horses and been away out for half the day, doing a wee bit of taxiing for himself, and everyday he would earn one and half times what a mill worker would make.' And the profits did not stop with the actual drivers. 'There were cart makers, coach makers, furriers, harness dressers and harness makers, and that is all linked to early taxiing in Belfast.'

However, with the advent of the motor-car in the late nineteenth century, the lucrative taxi trade would soon experience dramatic changes in the way it had to operate.

In 1896, John Brown Longhurst, a scientist of some repute who lived not far from Belfast, imported the first automobile into Ireland from France. His coal-fired Serpollet steam car would certainly have been a novel sight for the people of Belfast at the time, but Longhurst was continually frustrated by the condition of the Irish roads, and cabbies would no doubt have looked on in disdain as their horses outran and outmanoeuvred his noisy new contraption.

But less than a decade later – and thanks, in part, to the advances in pneumatic tyres brought about by John Boyd Dunlop in 1887 – there were around 160 motorised vehicles in Ireland. Such a luxurious method of transport was exclusive to the upper classes, of course, but the burgeoning popularity of cars, and the subsequent realisation that some form of regulation was necessary, led to the introduction of the 1903 Motor Car Act. Under its terms the speed limit was increased from 14 to 20 mph; drivers now had to be licensed; and motor cars had to be registered – causing one outraged car owner to protest against being 'numbered like convicts and labelled hackney carriages'. Because it related solely to motorized transport, the 1903 Act did not impose upon the horse-drawn taxi industry too much, but with motor cars gradually becoming more numerous in Ireland as the new century wore on, more Acts of Government relating to transport followed.

The Finance Acts of 1908 and 1909–10 enabled the government to improve roads in Ireland via taxation levied on petrol and against the horsepower of vehicles; the Motor Traffic Act of 1925 introduced the idea that a licence ought to contain the holder's photograph – an initiative that was made compulsory in Northern Ireland in 1926, while Great Britain would only follow suit in 1998, over seventy years later – but it was the Motor Vehicles (Traffic and Regulation) Act of 1926 (Northern Ireland) that would have the most impact on Northern Irish taxis in the early twentieth century.

Relating mostly to public service vehicles – defined in the Act as 'mechanically propelled vehicles used in standing or plying for hire or used to carry passengers for hire' – the 1926 Act required drivers to 'be clean and to wear a uniformed cap' under all circumstances, to have a copy of the by-laws on their person at all times and, most importantly, to fit their vehicle with a 'taximeter'. These meters ensured that all drivers adhered to the prescribed rates per mile. Drivers had to reset their taximeter to zero as soon as they were hired.

Geoff, a former taxi driver who worked for several unlicensed companies in the early part of his career, explained that taximeters have always been as important for drivers as for passengers: 'Before taximeters were introduced you just wouldn't have been able to make money. One day I lifted two wee ladies from the Royal hospital who were going to Oxford Street Bus Station. I was travelling down Chichester Street in a taxi without a meter and the traffic was stopped dead. I hadn't moved an inch and every half an hour the wee lady in the back would turn and say to the other one, "Mabel, what time's the next bus?" Mabel would say, "Oh, we're all right, there's another one at 4.30." Then at 4.30 Mabel would turn and say, "Ah, we missed that one. There's another one at 5." I could see the bus station, it was five-hundred yards away, but these two ladies weren't getting out of my car until I dropped them at the door. They were in my car for two and three-quarter hours and they only paid me £1.80! If I'd had a meter they'd have been up like Lazarus and away.'

As significant as those changes to taxiing were, it was the introduction of the Austin FX4 to the market in 1958 that would represent the biggest advance in the industry. Although there is no shortage of claim and counterclaim from taxi drivers in Belfast, it is not known exactly when the first hackney was imported from London to Belfast (estimates range from 1910 to the 1930s), but this familiar cab – commonly known in Northern Ireland as the 'black taxi' – would remain in continuous production for almost forty years and become the most famous and iconic of all taxis.

'When the traditional black taxi came on the scene in London,' said Joe, 'it opened up the doors for people who could access the money to buy one, not just in London but all around the UK and Ireland. They could buy independent employment. They didn't need to belong to a company, they

Items on Loan

Library name: Downpatrick
Library
User name: Mr Robert Duffy

Author: Henry, Lee.
Title: Belfast taxi : a drive
through history, one fare
Item ID: C701141616
Date due: 4/1/2022,23:59
Date charged: 7/12/2021,
18:19

LibrariesNI
****
Make your life easier
****
Email notifications are sent
two days before item due
dates
Ask staff to sign up for
email

could be self-employed, and if they had one or two sons they could even take it in turn to earn their living from the one vehicle. Black taxis cost a lot of money, but they done it [found the money for it]. They were a service to the public and also an independent livelihood for Protestant and Catholic alike.'

Having secured a suitable vehicle, public-hire cab drivers could then queue up for business at the various taxi ranks located around the city. 'There was a famous one in Garfield Street at the side of the GPO [General Post Office],' said Joe. 'There was one at City Hall, one round at Amelia Street, one outside the GNR [Great Northern Railway] and one at the LMS Railway. There were quite a lot of them, but you would never have seen a big long queue of taxis at stands then. Perhaps ... at the Garfield Street stand, because of the cinemas and all that, people coming out at night-time.'

It was the dawn of a new era for Belfast and her taxi drivers. Slowly but surely Belfast's taxis had become a mode of transport open to everyone, not just the privileged few.

Silver Cabs and the Private-hire Taxi Industry

> People didn't have cars in them days, they had to use us.
>
> RALPH McMURRAY
> *former director of Silver Cabs*

As the public taxi trade flourished in the early part of the twentieth century, the formation of a private-hire taxi industry in the late 1930s in Belfast was a natural progression. Rapid advances in telecommunications meant that it soon became possible for customers to pre-book their taxis, rather than having to queue up and wait in designated areas, and to have drivers pick them up or drop them off at any location they chose.

One particular company owner, William John McCausland, would soon set the example for all others to follow. During the First World War, McCausland – a former farm labourer from Ballymoney – was stationed in Ypres, France, as an ambulance driver, where he met his soon-to-be business partner, Ambrose Sydney Baird. Both men had a love of automobiles and an instinct for business, and they returned to Northern Ireland determined to utilise these skills to build a successful business.

In 1920 – after some years spent working as mechanics in Belfast, fixing automobiles for private individuals or haulage companies, sourcing parts and making contacts – they decided to go into business for themselves, and together formed the Progressive Motor Company. Based in premises on Carlton Street, on the southern edge of greater Belfast, McCausland and Baird began to hire out their own self-drive cars, and in time became associated with the first motoring school in Belfast, the W.J. McCausland Driving School.

It was a period of economic uncertainty and depression in Belfast, but their operation was so successful that it quickly outgrew the Carlton Street yard and, within a matter of months, they had moved into larger premises on the Grosvenor Road, Belfast, now trading as Baird & McCausland.

After two years of successful business, there was an amicable parting of the ways: Baird went on to open the extremely successful A.S. Baird car showrooms on the Boucher Road, while McCausland continued in car sales and rentals. McCausland's business boomed and, despite the upheaval caused by the onset of the Second World War, he opened Auto Taxis on 24 October 1939.

An astute businessman, McCausland understood the value of advertising and marketing, and the name Auto Taxis was chosen for a good reason – to appear high up in the phone book listings (a ploy that future company owners would emulate during the private-hire boom in the 1960s). The business gained momentum and a reputation as a reliable firm soon followed, with customers from all over the city using the company.

With few competitors in those early years and with a fleet made up of large, lumbering hackney cabs – mostly Morris and Ford models imported from London – Auto Taxis managed to survive the rigours of the Second World War, providing employment for around twenty drivers. It was a feat managed in part by an ingenious device that the ever-resourceful McCausland made use of to combat fuel shortages during wartime. With petrol rationing hampering the fleet's progress, McCausland decided to look for an alternative form of fuel to keep his cabs running. Drawing on his expertise in vehicle maintenance, he converted his cars to run on town gas, provided by suppliers at the gas works on the Ormeau Road, and fixed a canvas bag – 'like a tent', according to Joe Graham – to the roof of his cabs as storage for the new fuel.

To get the cars started, drivers had to lie underneath the vehicles and heat the oil in the engine with a blowtorch before turning the cars over using the gas. When the gas froze during the winter months, drivers often had to urinate on the sacks to heat them up.

It was obviously an extremely dangerous way to keep the cabs on the road, but was, nevertheless, an effective one. No accidents were ever reported to McCausland by any of his drivers, and after two years of running successfully on gas the Auto Taxis fleet returned to petrol when rationing was relaxed by the War Office.

Then, in 1942, McCausland decided to expand his business by adding a number of limousines to the fleet. He changed the company name to the more refined Silver Cabs, and even commissioned a radio advertisement – 'Phone 27444 and Silver Cabs will be at your door'.

As the years wore on Silver Cabs began to face competition from a number of smaller private-hire companies operating in various parts of the city – Anytime, Anywhere on Berry Street, Blue Line on Upper Library Street, and Star Taxis on the Antrim Road, for example – all of which had fleets of around six taxis. Their largest competitor at the time was Fast Taxis, which had its depot at Bridge End and employed around thirty drivers. Given the competition, McCausland was not inclined to rest on his laurels and, ever eager to grow his business and to outbid and outmanoeuvre his closest competitors, eventually he bought out all these firms.

In 1950, when McCausland (now known affectionately within the company as 'the Old Man') bought Anytime, Anywhere,

Silver Cabs also acquired a few members of staff. One man in particular, Ralph McMurray – who had been a telephone operator for Anytime, Anywhere – would go on to become one of Silver Cabs' most loyal and long-serving employees.

'William John was semi-retired when I went to work in the Grosvenor Road office,' recalled a smartly dressed Ralph on the day of our interview. 'He had given over the running of the business to two of his sons, Harold and William, but he would still come down to the office every morning for ten or fifteen minutes to look in and say hello. His sons would not have made any decisions without him.

'What kind of a man was he? Well, at that time – in the early 1950s – taxi drivers working for Silver Cabs could have been sacked if they were caught diddling – doing runs and not recording them and all that sort of thing. That was the Silver Cabs policy. So the drivers wanted to bring in a trade union to represent them. I remember negotiations going on for a long time with the trade unions. Eventually, William John agreed to meet with their representative. There was a big meeting at the Grosvenor Road office. The trade union boys came in to meet with William John and his four sons, Harold, William, Victor and Sydney.

'Back then there were stones steps leading up to the offices. They had their meeting and the next thing we knew a chair came flying down the stairs and William John threw this union guy out on his knees,' Ralph recalled with a chuckle. 'That was the sort of man he was. He kept very strict control of the company until he was quite elderly, well into his seventies.'

Ralph was twenty-nine when he became a telephonist for Silver Cabs. Born on 20 March 1921, he grew up in the Donegall Road and Lisburn Road areas of Belfast, and left school aged fourteen. 'I got a job, funnily enough, in Crawford's Horse and Cart [Crawford's Hauliers], so I was always into transport, in a way. Then I worked as a clerk for Mackie's, one of the biggest textile manufacturing companies in the world, on the Springfield Road, doing some book-keeping before I had an accident and broke my spine. After that I lay in hospital in a plaster cast for two years.

'When I came out again I got work as a timekeeper at Harland & Wolff, and then for my uncle, who had one of the first cheque trading companies in Belfast, before joining Anytime, Anywhere Taxis and moving to Silver Cabs. I wasn't a driver – I didn't get my driving licence until I was nearly fifty – I was a telephonist originally, but got more involved in the running of the business as time went on.'

Ralph was promoted to office manager at Silver Cabs, then operations manager, eventually becoming general manager. He manned the phones in the busy Grosvenor Road headquarters, did the books and generally kept the whole thing ticking over, while Silver Cabs was asserting itself as the primary private-hire firm in Belfast.

'Obviously there were times when we were quiet. Then, suddenly, you would know that it was raining outside because the phones started ringing. At busy times in the office we had twenty phones ringing at once, and when eventually we bought Fast Taxis and closed their offices, but had their number still operating, we were picking up phones and answering 'Silver Cabs! Fast Taxis!' It was bedlam, absolute bedlam.

'We tried to have signs or lights on the phones instead of the ringing tone, but we found that the clerks didn't answer them as quick. Still, there was a good family bond between everyone. We just got on with it. There was that drive. We were a family.'

The Grosvenor Road depot was a lively, bustling place during the peaceful days of the 1950s. Year round, commuters flocked to the busiest taxi depot in town, factory workers waiting patiently alongside barristers for the next available cab.

'At that time we had a huge clock outside, which you could

see up and down the street and that was a favourite meeting place for people,' said Ralph. 'During busy times, particularly around Christmas and January, people would come in to the waiting room to wait for a taxi home. Whether they were in rags or silks they just sat and took their time.'

Eventually, Silver Cabs came to employ around one hundred drivers, and became, as Ralph said, 'the big taxi company in the city'. There were, of course still the public-hire drivers – or 'street cars' as Ralph called them – to compete with, but the friction that exists between public and private-hire drivers today was not as evident during the 1950s.

'At that time the street cars would have gone down to the boats in the morning, with people going to visit families in England, and they would have filled the taxi with three or four different fares and charged them all,' recalled Ralph. 'The street cars then would have been very aggressive towards customers. There would have been verbal abuse between our drivers and the black taxis at times. But, generally, they were very friendly with us. Harold, William John's son, would have drank with them occasionally.

'There were not nearly as many street cars as there are now, but they would have used us, in a way. When we were busy and the waiting room was full, the street cars – which were allowed to pick up in the street – would have been back and forward picking up our passengers. We were glad to get rid of the surplus at busy times.'

Unlike today – when most private taxi firms in Belfast allow self-employed drivers to drive under a rank's banner – Silver Cabs employed its workforce directly, and paid drivers a small weekly wage. But the upmarket clientele who used Silver Cabs ensured that drivers went home of an evening with plenty of spare change in their pockets. 'The wages were low and generally everybody was struggling,' said Ralph. 'But many of our fares were wealthier men. Bookmakers, judges, solicitors, barristers, business people – they all used us, particularly in the evenings, and for the drivers the tips were very good.

'I've always remembered one particular chap who had never taxied before, but we gave him a chance. The wages, at that time, were probably around a fiver a week, and this new chap didn't lift his pay on the Friday, so we assumed he thought there was a lying week or something like that. The next Friday he didn't lift his pay either. So I asked him why. He said, "Do you get paid as well?"'

'Another driver used to say that it was the best job in the world. He could go out and get drunk, spend every penny, and know that with his first fare in the morning, he could go and buy cigarettes. But we had drivers who sent their sons to university to study as doctors, the ones who were careful and sensible.

'The taxman obviously carried out a few surveys. They said, "Right, you earn so much in tips," and they wanted to tax drivers. But there was no definitive proof when they assessed it. The drivers grumbled, but it wasn't anything to worry about.'

For the drivers themselves, finding work with one of the taxi companies in Belfast was not the difficult task it might have been in other major cities, like London, where prospective taxi drivers must take 'The Knowledge' – a demanding test that requires in-depth knowledge of London's streets, for which drivers take years to prepare. As a result Ralph was able to call upon drivers from various backgrounds and areas of the city: 'We had good drivers who were intelligent and could pick it up quick. They needed to have a PSV [Public Service Vehicle] licence, which was relatively easy to get in those days. We required our drivers to know the town, and there were wee booklets published by the city council that listed all the street names in Belfast. Many's a time the bell would ring, a driver would come to the window to collect a job, then he would drive round the corner, stop and get the booklet out, because he couldn't let us know that he didn't know where he was going.

'Women didn't drive taxis back then; it just wasn't the way

of things. But we had all kinds working for us, Catholics and Protestants. I remember we had two bank managers who had lost their jobs through alcohol or whatever, and they came and taxied for us.'

And there were other interesting individuals employed in the Silver Cabs fleet who had, or would in time, obtain notoriety as celebrities in the city.

Rinty Monaghan, the champion prizefighter from Belfast, drove for Silver Cabs in the latter half of the 1950s after hanging up his gloves some years before. 'Rinty was a character, no question about it,' said Ralph. 'I knew him when he was fighting during the war; I was in the casualty service and he was a driver in the motor pool. We were quite close at the time. He put on the gloves and would spar with anybody.

'Rinty used to train by letting down tyres on big lorries or ambulances, and pumping them up again. Letting them down, pumping them up. At the end of every fight he used to sing 'When Irish Eyes are Smiling', and at night time – on night duty when things were quiet – some of the other drivers would say, "Come on Rinty, sing us a song!" The only thing was, when you got him started you couldn't get him to stop, with that great deep voice of his. He was a performer, completely outgoing.

'There was another guy who worked for us for a while, a very spick-and-span, very neat boy named Jack Houston. I remember he always wore leather gloves. One day he went to the Old Man and asked permission to bring a friend into the waiting room during night duty. His name was James Young. They used to sit in the middle of the night, at three or four in the morning, and work on plays or sketches of theirs. James Young went on to become one of the most popular comedians in Northern Ireland, and when he started to take off, Houston didn't taxi anymore after that.'

James Young wasn't the only celebrity to grace the waiting room of Silver Cabs HQ. 'Brendan Behan came in one day,' Ralph recalled. 'He was in Belfast because of some play he had been writing or working on, but with him you wouldn't have known, he could have been doing anything.

'He wanted a taxi to Dublin, but at that time you just didn't just go across the border, you needed papers and everything. So we organised this and Behan entertained us while he was waiting. He had drink on him, shall I say. He was quite friendly and extrovert.

'So the driver took him. Obviously there was no motorway then, so it took a bit longer to get him to Dublin than it would today, but we didn't see the driver for three days after that! Evidently he had a great time; he got plenty of drink and he got well paid, but he fell out with the wife over it.'

Such journeys outside the city limits were not uncommon for Silver Cabs' drivers. 'I also remember a case when a couple of guys came in and wanted a taxi to go to Donegal so again we had to organise papers and for somebody to go over the border,' recollected Ralph. 'They wanted a roof rack on their taxi. Quite often you went on holidays with a roof rack back then. Eventually the driver came back to the depot and told us these guys had brought him to a house in Belfast. They went in and the next thing they came out with a big long box, wrapped blankets round it and put it on to the roof rack. They said, "Head for Letterkenny."

'I should say that, on the way up with the conversation and everything, the driver thought they were a bit rough. Anyway, he realised halfway there that this was a coffin on the roof with a body in it! But he was intimidated. He said he thought of stopping and calling a policeman or something, but there was not much he could do.

'When they got to Letterkenny there were two or three other cars waiting for them. He carried on and met these other guys and went in and had a few drinks and then went up this mountain road, very rocky, bendy and twisty. The cars weren't nearly as good in those days as they are now, but away up a remote mountain road he went, round the bend and so forth and the coffin came off and rolled down the hill!

That driver would never go to Donegal again. No way.'

Old Man McCausland and his staff were not too concerned about the peculiarities or morals of individual drivers, so long as they did not affect the drivers' work, so inevitably there was the odd questionable character on the books at Silver Cabs.

'One of our drivers, Billy, he was a bit of a lad,' mused Ralph. 'He messed about with girls, got a disease, was attending a clinic in the Royal Hospital, recognised one of the patients, who was quite well known – I think he was a barrister – and decided to blackmail him. Obviously the barrister had got a disease too – he was attending a VD clinic, after all. So the driver approached him and threatened to let his wife know, but the barrister called the police and our driver was charged with blackmail. In the end he got two or three months for it.

'Then, one night at four o'clock in the morning the door to the waiting room at the Grosvenor Road office opened, this young woman ushered in two or three children and shouted into us, "Tell Billy to come and collect his children, I'm not going to mind them anymore, I'm away." She did a runner. It was this same driver's wife!

'He found out afterwards that she was pregnant with his child, but that their neighbours on either side of them were also pregnant, and all to him! I don't know what he did with the children. He must have brought them to his mother or whatever. But he was with us for months after that until he did the time. He never came back after that.'

Silver Cabs was a strictly non-sectarian outfit, and although simmering tensions existed in Belfast between the two communities, drivers of all backgrounds could drive into all areas of the city. There were occasional riots and disturbances that made drivers nervous, yet Ralph found it difficult to recollect any instances of violence perpetrated by members of the Belfast public on Silver Cabs' drivers.

'The only violence I ever saw was at Christmas, when everyone was drunk and wanted to get home and we hadn't the cars to accommodate all of them. I remember we had a clerk who used to look out at them all shouting at each other and say, "Look at them: they're celebrating the birth of Christ!"'

If Ralph and his crew couldn't quieten down the punters themselves, they could always rely on others to help. Then, as now, Belfast was never short of a hard man to keep the rowdy mob in check. 'Have you ever heard of Silver McKee?' asked Ralph. 'Silver McKee was an infamous character, a real hard man; he was a Catholic from the Markets area and was in and out of jail all the time. He had been a cattle drover. We got to know him; obviously he used to come in to use taxis and so forth. Round about Christmas, when people were getting really rowdy, if he happened to come in he would say, "Sit you effin' down there!" and anyone that knew him did as he said.'

Silver Cabs also boasted a clientele that was as varied as its staff. Bookmakers, judges, solicitors and barristers would use taxis for personal transport, and also for other less than savoury pursuits, as Ralph explained with a wicked glint in his eye.

'You'd be surprised at some of the people that used prostitutes. Obviously there were affairs going on. Solicitors and judges would have rung our office and said, "Right, get a bottle of whiskey and a girl and bring her up." And the driver went and got the whiskey or whatever and collected the girl and brought her up the Antrim Road.

'Prostitutes would have come into our waiting room to get a taxi when they had finished their shift, so you got to know quite a few. Most of them were very generous, decent girls. Some of them would come in and maybe they'd be broke because they just drank everything, and they would say, "Do you trust me until tomorrow night?" They always came back and paid their fare.'

Of course, not everyone could afford to use taxis all of the time. For working-class people using taxis as transport was often limited to special occasions. If there was an emergency, for example, taxis were often the only form of transport reliable enough to get fares to the chapel, or indeed to the hospital, on time.

'Because people didn't have cars in them days, they had to use us,' confirmed Ralph. 'We had limousines and used to do a lot of weddings in my day, up at Belfast Castle, the Woodburn Hotel, Crawfordsburn Inn, places like that. On one occasion I remember we sent the driver for the groom to take him to the church. The driver got there but the groom had been drinking the night before, he wasn't up or shaved and the driver had to help him dress. He told him he had to go next door to borrow a pair of cuff links and he radioed into us – the bride was already on the way to the church in another of our cars! So the driver who had the bride had to circle and circle around town until we got the groom there. Then we had to change our policy. Unless it was absolutely impractical because of distance we always used the one car for weddings. We went for the groom, dropped him at the church and then we went for the bride.

'There was another occasion, a maternity case, and the girl was quick. I don't know what happened exactly, but the baby was born right there in the taxi before they got to the hospital! A wee girl. The next day the girl's parents came in to the office with an envelope for the driver and told us that they had called the baby Sylvia after Silver Cabs. Years later a young girl came in and introduced herself as Sylvia. Things like that happened all the time.'

In time Silver Cabs became a part of the furniture in Belfast. Throughout the 1950s it had prided itself on being the largest taxi firm in Belfast, but it was also the most progressive. The McCauslands were the first operators in Belfast to install two-way radios in their cabs – even before the police. These radios were so bulky that they took up almost the entire boot of the car, remembers Ralph, but radio contact between operators and drivers allowed drivers to skip from job to job without returning to HQ for orders. For the first time, operators in dispatch could check on drivers from a distance and assign jobs in the vicinity.

Silver Cabs also had strict rules to which drivers were expected to adhere to keep the firm's reputation intact: an admirable system which has since, regrettably, fallen out of fashion with most companies in the city.

'Silver Cabs had a uniform, and drivers had to wear their caps all the time,' Ralph remarked. 'When they got to the customer's address they had to get out of the cab, go to the door and ring the bell or knock, then open the car door for the customer and so forth. There was none of this beeping the horn, as they do now,' he grumbled – truly a member of the old guard.

As Old Man McCausland began to take a back seat in the running of the company, his sons, Harold, William, Victor and Sydney took control of various aspects of the family business. Ralph enjoyed working with all of them, though remembers Harold as the dominant figure of the four.

'They were all well educated, but Harold was the one with the real brains. Although he went to Methodist College, he could barely write grammatically, but he was able to employ people. He had a head for business.

'I remember one time I was doing about ten sets of books for different companies and we had a weekly meeting. I said, "We're down two thousand pounds," or something like that, and he said, "Run that past me again." He queried it. "No, that's wrong. Last week it was such and such and we made so much." I checked the figures and he was right. He was very astute.'

Like his father before him, Harold was an imposing figure. He took his responsibilities within the family business very seriously, as well as the profit margins. His wrath was to be avoided at all costs. As general manager, however, Ralph enjoyed a close and respectful working relationship with the eldest of the Old Man's sons.

'In the early days Harold would come in to the office in the mornings for a report on the night before, and accidents were a real problem. I remember telling him one time "Paddy Magee had an accident and it's bad." He asked, "What happened?" "He ran into a ship." He actually had an accident with a ship!' Ralph continued, laughing. 'Paddy had dropped people down at the docks somewhere. He was driving along near a moored ship, which was obviously very close, didn't see it, hit the cement gangway and banged into the ship. But the reaction from the boss was okay when I told him, because we had a good bond. Obviously as I got up the ladder I became much more friendly with the McCauslands, working with them rather than for them.'

Although most drivers working for Silver Cabs were happy with their lot, a section of the workforce remained unhappy with the money they were making. The trade union continued to put pressure on William John, and Harold in turn, to improve the wage structure. And so, when the Old Man finally hung up his keys and handed the running of the company over to Harold completely, it was time for a fresh start.

Silver Cabs closed in 1961 and each of the four McCausland sons set up their own car business, with varying degrees of success. In the end, however, it was Harold's Belfast Car Hire, also located on the Grosvenor Road, that proved to be the most profitable. Harold was able to buy out the short-lived businesses started by William and Victor, and eventually even Sydney's more successful McCausland Car Hire, the name of which he kept.

All the while, Ralph stayed employed within the McCausland fold, moving between the brothers' various enterprises as the companies changed ownership. He thrived under Harold's stewardship, first becoming general manager of Belfast Car Hire before being made manager of Harold's McCausland Car Hire and a fully paid-up member of the

Board of Directors. He worked as company secretary and fulfilled duties as financial director until his retirement in January 1981.

The Troubles Begin

Don't stand there, son. You'll get shot.

DAVID McCRACKEN
former owner of Enterprise Taxis

By the 1960s, Belfast was thriving. The city had a vibrant music scene, with bands such as Van Morrison's Them, or Rory Gallagher and Taste championing the sounds of the decade in clubs like the Boom Boom Room on High Street. The 'fifth Beatle', George Best, was a bona fide home-grown pin-up, and post-Beat Generation poets, painters and activists flooded the corridors of Queen's University.

But Belfast was, at its core, a conservative, hard-working city, even during the 'Swinging Sixties'. Both Protestant and Catholic clergy remained influential, and church attendance was consistently high; old industries were making way for new, with engineering, as ever, providing the bulk of the jobs. For most of the 1960s, Belfast was a relatively stable and peaceful city.

For David McCracken – whose father, Andrew James McCracken, had established Enterprise Taxis in an office on the Albertbridge Road, east Belfast, on 13 December 1963 – the 1960s meant finishing school, learning to drive and getting used to working in a taxi dispatch office.

'In fact,' said David, who was only nine years old when

25

Enterprise was formed, 'I helped my dad to decorate the Enterprise Taxis office when they were getting ready to open up in 1963. And in 1965, when my dad – who had a history of ill health – was in hospital for a week, I went down and worked on the desk. I was always there to help from I was a nipper. And in my early teens I always worked Sunday evenings or Saturday mornings, helping out over the weekend when I wasn't at school.'

Like so many taxi drivers in Belfast whose fathers or brothers happened to have a PSV licence, taxiing was an obvious career choice for David. He admits that he thought about pursuing other careers, but, in the end, he decided to work alongside his father, with whom he enjoyed a very close relationship.

'I don't ever remember making a conscious decision to be a taxi man,' he explained, 'but I remember making a conscious decision that I wanted to work with my dad. My dad and I got on very well together; it was a family business. I didn't want to do anything else. So when I left school I started working in the office full-time. And when they changed the age for getting your PSV licence from twenty-one to nineteen years of age [in 1973], I started taxiing. I was the youngest taxi driver in Belfast at that time, the first legal nineteen-year old taxi driver in the city. Although,' he confessed sheepishly, 'like a whole lot of others, I had been taxiing before that.'

But Belfast had changed drastically in the ten years between Enterprise opening its doors and David acquiring his licence. As the decade had progressed, tensions between the nationalist and unionist communities had begun to manifest themselves in worrying ways.

Since 1964, and led by groups like Campaign for Social Justice (CSJ), which eventually became the Northern Ireland Civil Rights Association (NICRA), there had been a growing campaign for equality in Northern Ireland. Frustrated by the discriminatory policies imposed by the Stormont government, which was dominated by diehard unionist politicians, nationalist politicans and community representatives sought to end the discrimination suffered by Catholics in housing, employment and through gerrymandering.

On 17 April 1966, in reaction to this, and sparked by a series of republican parades in Belfast which marked the fiftieth anniversary of the Easter Rising, the Ulster Volunteer Force (UVF), a Loyalist paramilitary group, officially declared war on the Irish Republican Army (IRA) – who had fought for a United Ireland in the 1920s, 40s and 50s. In the weeks that followed, the UVF shot dead three civilians and wounded two others.

In 1968, marches organised by NICRA in Derry led to violent clashes between demonstrators and the Royal Ulster Constabulary (RUC). And in 1969, following the Battle of the Bogside – when the RUC attempted to disperse a group of nationalists who were protesting against a loyalist Apprentice Boys parade in Derry – violence flared across the country, and Northern Ireland once again descended into bloody sectarian conflict.

Despite the increasing sectarian tensions, the Belfast taxi industry kicked up a gear during the 1960s. In the 1960 *Belfast Street Directory*, there were forty entries listed under 'Taxi and Motorcar Hirers', including companies like Auto Taxis and York Taxis, as well as private individuals, like Fred Freeman of Houston Park or S.J. Campbell of Hewitt Parade. By 1969, the *Belfast Street Directory* listed forty-six entries under the same heading, but these included fewer private individuals and more firms employing crews of drivers, like the newly established King's Taxi and Car Hire, amongst others.

Ralph, who had enjoyed the relative peace of the 1950s with Silver Cabs and the prosperity of the 1960s working for Harold McCausland, experienced first-hand how the Troubles affected the taxi industry.

'I remember a couple of times in the late 1960s and early 1970s going down to the office and finding that the army was outside and a bomb was inside. We were robbed a few times too. It was all part of the economic war, the paramilitaries just causing disruption in Belfast.

'Guys came into the office wearing balaclavas and put a gun to my head half a dozen times. But the most frightening occasion was when three or four guys came in with sub-machine guns wearing Mickey Mouse and Donald Duck masks. I don't like being intimidated, but those masks were far more frightening and intimidating than balaclavas.'

For a man who had lived through the devastation caused by the Belfast Blitz, the Troubles came as a massive shock to Ralph. He still walked to work in the mornings as before – dressed smartly, a thin, sprightly man propelled by a firm work ethic – and watched in dismay as the city began to disintegrate around him. Like many others, he kept to his routine and prayed that the bloodshed would soon be over, but no one in Belfast was exempt from the trauma.

'It was crazy,' Ralph continued. 'I thought about leaving fonaCAB, for my family, but I couldn't get as good a position or a job as well paid. And I remember we had a few laughs. One day this old man rang us and said that he'd left an umbrella in the office,' said Ralph. 'We looked around, found the umbrella and told him to come down and get it. Then, this gang came in: three or four of them in balaclavas with sub-machine guns. They had us all up against the back wall, behind the counter, holding us while the safe was being done next door.

'In the middle of all this, the wee man walks in, goes up to the counter and says, "I don't want a taxi. I'm down about my umbrella." He had no idea what was going on around him! We caught on and said, "Get in here." But one of gunmen came out from the back, pointed the gun at him and said,

"Do you see that?" The old man looked at the gun and said, "No, mine was a long one." He thought it was an umbrella! Even the fellas with the guns burst out laughing.'

Such stories are common amongst Belfast taxi drivers, who seem to have an innate talent for spotting the humour in the darkest of circumstances. Ciaran – a driver interviewed at the annual Taxi and PSV Magazine Show in Belfast's King's Hall – related perhaps the most bizarre story from that period.

'I was in a taxi depot one night and these three guys came in looking a taxi, said they were going to a certain place, blah, blah, blah, and they got into the car. Then they said, "We're the Provisional IRA and we're taking this vehicle to use in a punishment shooting. We'll be taking you to premises where you'll be held for a short time. The car will be returned to you undamaged." So what happened was, they brought me to this basement, and when I got there, there was a guy who was going to be holding me. By God,' he said, pausing for dramatic effect, 'it turned out he was my cousin!

'Well he near had a nervous breakdown – so did I, because I didn't even know he was involved in anything like that. "You may just sit down there and we'll have a yarn," he said, and he made me a cup of tea. What do you do, like? It was mad.

'After a couple of hours they brought the car back and they said, "Don't be reporting this for two hours." I went to the police and they said, "That's OK, we'll look into it." But they never did. I never heard another thing about it. I spoke to my cousin later. He said, "Listen, just forget about it. It's over now, don't be worrying."'

James – a successful private-hire company owner and former driver – explained why Ciaran, and many other victims of paramilitary activity at the time, rarely reported such incidents to the police. Drivers were trying to protect themselves against possible paramilitary retribution, should their attackers be identified and charged, so many of these 'minor incidents', as he termed them, went unreported and unpunished.

'There were a lot of things that you didn't report, because you were putting yourself in the position where you then had to ID people,' James explained. 'If you're a taxi driver moving in and out of these areas, your career was over if you identified somebody, or went in to court as a witness … I suppose it depended on your outlook. If you got your car back, you didn't pursue it any further.'

But those 'minor incidents' were not the worst that could happen to drivers, or their depots. 'Our office got petrol bombed,' David McCracken told me, 'and the pub, our Enterprise taxi depot and wee Mr Thompson's sweetie shop on the bottom of the Ravenhill Road all burnt down that night. Those buildings disappeared and so we moved to a tailor's shop in Madrid Street that had just become vacant. My father ran the business from there and stayed there until the early 1980s.

'Things at that particular time were quite bad, trouble-wise, around the town and the new office was no safer. We were more or less beside the Short Strand [one of the most volatile front lines in Belfast], facing the Ravenhill Road, and there were endless fights inside the office. Somebody would come in and say they were going to a particular part of town, with people sitting there going to a politically opposite part of the town. The next thing, they had fisticuffs.'

Despite this, Enterprise was determined to remain neutral, employing drivers from both sides of the political divide and serving a large cross-section of the community. 'We tried very, very hard to be a totally non-sectarian company,' David explained, speaking for his father. 'We didn't care anything about what religion you were; we were more interested in whether or not you got out of your bed to come into work.'

Enterprise had one employee at this time who was not only able to get out of bed to get into work; he was also one of Belfast's most famous faces – singer and comedian Roy Walker, who would go on to win the ITV talent show *New*

Faces in 1977 and become host of the much-loved game show *Catchphrase* in 1986.

Originally from the Woodstock Road in east Belfast, close to the original Enterprise office, Walker had already made his name in Belfast in the late 1960s and early 1970s as compère of The Talk of the Town, a popular nightclub and music hall at Bridge End. Big bands and cabaret were all the rage at that time, and the multi-talented Walker remembers working with other artists at The Talk of the Town during its heyday in the mid-1960s.

'We had a band and we sang the hit parade and filled in with a few jokes, and got people up to play different games like Take Your Pick. We opened with all sorts of English cabaret stars, like Johnny Valentine. I saw integration happening between Catholics and Protestants gradually in the Talk of the Town. But then the Troubles came.'

On 1 September 1971 a bomb exploded in The Talk of the Town. As the damage was being repaired, Walker and the club's crew of entertainers found themselves out of work.

'I had a wee grocery shop on the Woodstock and what have you,' recalled Walker. 'It was doing really badly, and I wasn't working cabaret at night, but I was determined to work. There was a fella called Derek who was a taxi driver. His wife was a hairdresser, and they used to sit in the front row at The Talk of the Town every Monday night. They never missed it. When the Troubles kicked off, and The Talk of the Town was blown up, Derek said to me, "What are you going to do, Roy? I'm sure it'll blow over quick, but if you want a job as a taxi driver, I'll put your name forward." So I found myself working for Enterprise. I worked as a taxi driver for about a year. It really was as easy as that. I had a car and I just started taxiing.

'Enterprise was great. It was mixed, and I could go anywhere. I had been compère at Talk of the Town, had been in the paper almost every week, so I was very well known. I would pull up to collect a passenger at the barricades and they would joke with me, "Aw, here he is. The crap singer!" But I didn't mind that I was forced to taxi. I like people, you see; I used to sing for them and everything.

'One of our jobs in Belfast was to take disabled children to school every morning. There was one lovely wee girl who I used to taxi, and we used to sing and harmonise together. After I stopped taxiing and moved to England, I never saw her after that. Lo and behold, years later her daughter came up to me after one of my shows in Edinburgh and said, "My mammy remembers you from when you drove the taxi. She always said you were a great singer."'

Despite Walker's popularity in east Belfast, being married to a Catholic inevitably drew the attention of the paramilitaries. A gunman and his accomplice approached him in the street one day, called him a 'Fenian lover' and demanded that he vacate the city within twenty-four hours.

Walker posted a sign in the window of his grocery shop, which read, 'The owner of this shop served Queen and country for six years', before boarding a ship to England. The paramilitaries decided to firebomb his grocery shop nevertheless.

It was a time when being seen to fraternise with 'the enemy' could cost you your livelihood and, in some cases, your life, but David believes that Enterprise's non-sectarian policy actually prevented any further attacks on their premises. 'We went everywhere, literally,' he explained. 'We drove people to any part of Belfast … And I think, to a certain extent, that kept our office safe, because people knew that we worked both sides of the street. We were left alone in comparison to some other companies.'

However, the Enterprise fleet was another matter. In all probability, Enterprise's policy actually increased the likelihood that their taxis would fall victim to paramilitary attacks, given their drivers' willingness to travel into the most hardline areas. This was also the case for other legitimate taxi companies that served all areas of Belfast.

'I remember stopping on the Woodstock Road in the early 1970s, rapping the door to take a lady up to the Ulster Hospital and wondering what those funny zinging noises were,' David recalled, laughing at the memory. 'Of course, there was a gun battle going on between the Woodstock Road and Woodstock Street, which was close to the Short Strand. The paramilitaries were shooting at each other and I could hear the bullets, but, because it was the first time that I'd heard them, I had no idea that that's what they were.

'I was standing outside, rapping at the door, when it opened and some woman came out and trailed me in, saying, "Don't stand there, son. You'll get shot." Then two fellas got behind my car, using it as cover to shoot down into Woodstock Street. I thought, "To hell with this, those fuckers are going to see them and shoot back and they'll hit my car." So I ran out, got into the car and drove off.

'We had a lot of other drivers get into bother during the Troubles; we had endless cars hijacked,' said David. 'I remember one time my father went away for a fortnight for a summer holiday and during that time we managed to lose eight cars! They were hijacked, taken off different drivers, most of them blown up.

'One of the drivers, they put a hood put over his head and some so-and-so sat and clicked a gun in his ear for the next hour. His nerves were wrecked; he couldn't do any taxiing again after that for a long, long time.

'The last one hijacked was left outside Telephone House on Cromac Street. I actually ran through the army cordon to get to it. I opened the boot and the bonnet before the robot got there to blow the thing up, because I just couldn't stand the thought of losing another car. My dad was coming home in two days and I didn't want to tell him there was another car lost. Nerves are a shocking thing; they can get you into awful situations. But it wasn't booby-trapped, thank God.

'I even got hijacked myself once,' David added with a smile. 'It was a Monday morning at 9.30 a.m. exactly. They got a hold of my car and said, "Don't do anything silly, there's no reason to." There was no violence or anything like that; they were very nice and polite the whole way through.

'I was supposed to spend the next hour in St. Paul's Chapel to wait for them to come back and let me know where the car was. I stuck it for about ten minutes, just getting more and more frustrated. Obviously, I wanted to let the office know that I was all right. So I got up to leave the chapel with every intention of finding a pay phone, and when I got up half the congregation got up with me! There was a bunch of wee lads in the chapel and they were all watching to make sure I stayed there.

'Then, a young lad handed me a bit of paper saying, "Your car is in Linden Street." It was just down the Falls Road a wee bit. I went down and the car was sitting there with the keys in the ignition. They must have been using it to ferry stuff around. I got into my car and was back in work an hour and a half later.'

Being a hearty, healthy young twenty-something at the time, perhaps David was able to deal with such episodes without letting them affect his ability to work. And yet, as the violence continued and the destructive efforts of the paramilitaries increased, even young men like David were not able to remove themselves from the emotional impact of the conflict with such ease.

Shortly after the outbreak of the Troubles, the IRA adopted an economic warfare strategy that saw them detonate explosive devices in hotels, bus and rail stations, civil service buildings and retail premises in the centre of town on a sickeningly regular basis. The aim: to stop the Northern Irish economy in its tracks and encourage the British government to cut ties.

David remembers the worst example of this trend, Bloody Friday, when on 21 July 1972 the IRA detonated twenty-two bombs within a 75-minute period in the centre of Belfast. Nine people were killed and one hundred and thirty people injured. It was one of the darkest days in the history of Belfast, and one that many Belfast taxi drivers will never forget.

'All the bombs went off in Belfast that day,' David recalled. 'It was awful. People didn't go anywhere for weeks after that, because of the fear factor. Taxi work ceased, it just stopped dead. Taxi men just stood around and looked at each other.'

There was little else for them to do. The city that many of those taxi drivers had grown up in was now the epicentre of a brutal conflict. The highest annual death toll of the Troubles was recorded that year with 496 murders, and 258 of those victims categorised as civilians. On 21 April 1974, another terrible milestone came: the thousandth victim of the Troubles, James Murphy, was found dead on a roadside in County Fermanagh. The tide of violence seemed unstoppable.

While some taxi drivers chose to quit the profession and move out of Belfast at this time, others attempted to adapt to their changing environment. They had a difficult road ahead.

Taxiing Through the Troubles

What was going through your mind when you picked somebody up? Is this going to be my last fare? Maybe you were going to get one in the back of the head. That's you, away to the heavens above.

RONNIE
former soldier and taxi driver

Central Belfast during the height of the Troubles was nothing like it is today. Younger generations undoubtedly take their vibrant, cosmopolitan capital for granted, but throughout the 1970s and 1980s – and even into the 1990s – Belfast was not a safe place to be.

There were bomb alerts daily, hoax calls that led to the security forces having to block off roads and clear buildings of employees, and synchronised explosions designed to cause maximum disruption, stretch the security services, and to injure, maim and kill en masse.

'It was quite volatile then, to say the least,' former taxi driver James explained. 'By about six or seven o'clock at night, the town was completely closed up. A lot of the businesses, pubs and restaurants in particular, were virtually non-existent in the city centre after eight o'clock at night. So people stayed in their own areas.

'The city centre at that time was enclosed by a ring of steel, as they used to call it. It was sealed off and security personnel manned all four approaches into the city centre. There were security checks at Donegall Place, opposite the City Hall, which was the main route into the city, as well as at the top of High Street, Castle Street, and on Royal Avenue.'

There were security checks for pedestrians too. 'There were turnstiles. You could get out, but you couldn't get back in through them. Cars were not allowed in, unless they were pulled apart and checked first.'

And the entrances to the ring of steel were not the only security points in Belfast at that time. Throughout the 1970s and 1980s there were impromptu checkpoints all over the city.

'The security checkpoints were on every major route into the town,' confirmed James. 'They might have been there for an hour, depending, I suppose, on what information they had with regards to vehicles being taken into the town, or who they were looking for.'

But rather than feel perturbed or affronted by such checkpoints, most taxi drivers in Belfast – aside, of course, from the most fervent republicans – looked to the security checkpoints for protection at times of uncertainty.

'If you knew there was trouble in a particular area and your passenger wanted to go to that area, you would generally have dropped them at the nearest point and said, "Look I'm not going any further, you can walk it from here." That was just part of the business,' said James.

The checkpoints were also reassuring if a driver felt uncomfortable with, or intimidated by their passengers. 'If they had been up to anything these guys wouldn't have moved if they thought there was a security block ahead. A lot of times, if you were in a hurry to get somewhere, they were a hindrance. They could cause serious tailbacks. But if they were about, it was a bit of a safety net for you.'

One man I interviewed, Ronnie – who became a taxi

driver himself in the late 1990s – was actually one of the soldiers who manned those security checkpoints in the latter half of the Troubles.

Born and raised in Belfast, Ronnie witnessed the impact that the Troubles had on the taxi industry with his own eyes. He recalled crime scenes where taxi drivers had been murdered, and argued that 'everybody thinks taxiing is a great job, but it's a dangerous job. Believe me. I was in the Ulster Defence Regiment and the Royal Irish Regiment. I was on the streets of Belfast for seventeen years. I was in south Armagh and Crossmaglen and all that there as well, but mainly Belfast. And over the years, being in the forces, I saw a lot of taxi drivers shot dead, five-hundred pound bombs put in cabs, all sorts.

'Back then, there was a feud going on between the paramilitaries and taxi drivers were getting shot. You know, a Protestant and a Catholic, you shoot one, we'll shoot one. Tit for tat. It put a lot of people off taxiing, so it did.

'I would say that, for anybody who was taxiing during the Troubles, it must have been really, really hard for them. It's their livelihood, but what was going through your mind when you picked somebody up? Is this going to be my last fare? Maybe you were going to get one in the back of the head. That's you, away to the heavens above. They must have been crapping themselves.'

Where a taxi depot was located often determined who worked there. Smaller, locally-based taxi companies – particularly those found in hard-line areas in the west, east and north of the city – often employed drivers from their immediate area. So, generally speaking, a firm in a Catholic area would have mostly Catholic employees and a firm in a Protestant area would have mostly Protestant employees. Paramilitaries, therefore, could make an educated guess about a driver's religion based on where he or she worked.

'There were quite a few drivers that were set up through people knowing what taxi depot that they worked for,' said James. Like many drivers of the old school, he could not easily forget the pervasive influence that the paramilitaries had had over the people of the city.

'The likes of the city centre firms, there would have been a whole mixed crew in them, so some of the guys would have preferred to work there,' he continued, 'because no one would have been able to associate them with one side of the community or say exactly what religion they were. But other firms, where they were located, there were nearly all Protestants or all Catholics working in them. As a sectarian thing, the paramilitaries could have done it quite easy, just picked a driver, you know. If they wanted to shoot a Protestant, they knew strictly – "Well, that's that taxi depot there."'

James knew several taxi drivers who were murdered in Belfast as a result of this tactic. He would not give their names, nor talk in any great depth about them as individuals, but he did describe them as friends, as innocent victims.

'There was one guy who worked with me who left the depot and went to work in another firm in Glengall Street. I hadn't seen him for a spell and then I met him one day on the Woodstock Road,' said James. 'I spoke to him, and about a week later I heard it on the early morning news: a taxi had been found in Glencairn, and there was a fatality. It mentioned the name of the taxi firm, and he was the only one that I knew who worked in it. I wondered could it be him.

'Of course, it was him. Seemingly he'd picked up a fare at the taxi depot: couple of guys and a girl. He took the girl as well and dropped her about the Donegall Road somewhere, and that was the last … He was found, the car was burnt out and he was shot dead.

'Then there was another lad who I knew. He was away in England, working back and forth. His job had finished and he decided to do a bit of taxiing for a while. He got a call one night to Dunluce Avenue, I think it was, at the bottom of the Lisburn Road. He went down to the house and somebody ran out and shot him dead. They'd obviously known what religion he was.'

James still finds it difficult to accept that ordinary, hardworking men who had families to feed and who were not, as far as he was aware, in any way connected with the paramilitaries, were targeted by paramilitary assassins in such a cowardly, indiscriminate fashion.

Thirty-two taxi drivers in total were killed in Northern Ireland during the Troubles – twenty in Belfast itself – by murderers of both political persuasions, and many more were scarred physically or emotionally by attacks on their person or vehicles. But through the darkest days there were still drivers who continued to work and refused to be deterred from doing the job that they loved.

But providing transport for a populace in the throes of a violent conflict meant that taxi drivers in Belfast faced new challenges. They were, after all, easy targets – they worked alone, they travelled to wherever their fares requested they travel, and they operated without the sophisticated digital equipment that they rely on today.

If the industry was to survive, it needed to adapt: the old ways had become untenable. Across the board, new safeguards were put in place to help protect drivers from attacks on their person. They did not guarantee the drivers' safety, but they helped.

'A lot of the taxi firms are now computerised, but in those days it was all radio,' James explained. 'So operators used drivers' numbers when they were assigning jobs, strictly no names, because if they used someone's name across the radio – Billy or Paddy – the passengers could have identified where the driver was from. If someone's calling your name out over a radio and you respond to it, you could have put yourself in a bit of trouble. A number didn't mean anything.'

Drivers also learned to work together to avoid trouble. With Belfast becoming ever more segregated, there were certain areas of the city that were deemed more dangerous to enter than others. These areas – main thoroughfares like the Falls and Shankill roads, or hardline estates like loyalist Tiger's Bay in north Belfast or nationalist Andersonstown in the west, for example – were often the scene of gun battles, violent riots, marches or other demonstrations. Maintaining communication between drivers from all quarters of the city was vital. Information was passed via radio and telephone, or in person in depots, cafes, or at ranks throughout the city.

Derek – a driver I interviewed at the Taxi and PSV Magazine Show in the King's Hall – explained the importance of developing contacts within the taxi industry and expanding your support network to help ensure that you got home safe and sound at the end of the working day.

'The thing about taxiing in Belfast back then was that you couldn't go taxiing unless you knew the city,' said Derek. 'And, even if you knew the city, you needed to know at least eight men that you could count on, ones you could trust and ask what the story is. Other drivers would update you about different parts of the city that you didn't know. You were given warnings, you know. And the depots knew if something happened too, so you knew to stay away. They all worked together. "What's it like there?" "I'm not sure, but hold on. This guy lives there, I'll ring him and find out" "Stay away from Rathcoole, there's trouble on."

'That local information wasn't given out on the news, it was all word of mouth. If there was a problem or something going on downtown, you needed to know for your own safety, because, at the end of the day, you're out there on your own. There is nobody else. What are you going to do? It doesn't matter about police or army, they're few and far between. When you're out on the road, you have to think of yourself.'

In the midst of the violence private-hire firms dotted across the inner and outer city still managed to carry on and provide employment for hundreds of taxi drivers. Enterprise Taxis, for instance, survived on account jobs with large businesses and the Belfast residents' compulsion to escape the city when the chance arose.

'In those days there were maybe three-hundred taxi drivers in the entire city, and you really didn't need more than that,' explained David. 'You couldn't have gone into the city centre for entertainment anyway – it was better avoided. So people looked to head out of town, to places like Coachman's Inn in Bangor, because people felt safe in places like that, away from the danger that was inherent in Belfast city centre.

'Enterprise always looked for account work, because account work is safe. You don't have to collect fares off anybody, nobody's going to try to rob you or do your kneecaps, because account jobs are bona fide customers. That kept us safe, and in those days gave us a good backbone of work.

'We did work for the Eastern Health and Social Services, for example, and their health centre down the Holywood Road, which was opened to deal with stroke victims. But the number of people that we took there who had lost limbs in bomb blasts – being retrained to walk after they'd been fitted with artificial legs, crutches or whatever – was phenomenal. It really was quite scary. We were on the front line. We have probably seen slightly more than ordinary folk would have seen or experienced … but everybody was in the same boat. People taking a shot at you, or trying to take your car off you or looking to do your kneecaps, it was not that different from what the general population was experiencing … if you were living in some of the estates in different parts of the city you'd have been getting that on a daily, nightly basis.'

Working with the Press

There wasn't much point standing behind
people when they were the ones throwing
stones, because you couldn't see the anger. You
couldn't see the petrol bombs being lit.

CHARLIE O'BRIEN
former taxi driver and driver for the media

Life during the Troubles certainly wasn't easy, and many
drivers did their utmost to stay out of the hot spots and
avoid the danger. But there were some who experienced the
Troubles from close up. Charlie O'Brien – who worked as a
dispatcher for a private-hire firm at the time of interview, but
who has since retired – belongs to the latter group because he
worked, for a time at least, almost exclusively with the press.

I met Charlie quite a few times before he agreed to be
interviewed. He isn't a difficult character or antisocial in any
way – it was just that the stories he had weren't easy to tell.
He finally agreed to speak to me at the dispatch office where
he worked.

'I was born in Belfast on the Albertbridge Road way back
in 1952,' he began. 'I always worked in and around the
taxi industry, even when I was still at school. I was about
fifteen when I started ... My father before me worked for
Silver Cabs during the Second World War and my two elder

brothers worked for Enterprise. And when I got my licence and did my PSV test I started working with Enterprise as a motor mechanic. I used to come in and do the radio too.'

With taxiing in his blood, it was an obvious vocation and Charlie learned the ropes over the next few years, taxiing at a time when it was generally safe to do so. 'It was quiet then, there was no hassle in Belfast at that stage,' he recalled. 'Then all hell broke loose. There was rioting everywhere and that was the start of it. Nearly every day they tried to shoot somebody. They'd have rung up for a car, the driver took it, they got in and the next thing a gun was stuck in your ear.

'It happened to me once in the middle of Shaftesbury Square – 12 p.m. in the day, two guys standing in painters' overalls with kit bags. I asked, "Where are you heading?" "Ballymurphy," they said. Up the Donegall Road, up into Ballymurphy, and the next thing a gun comes in from the back seat under my fuckin' ribs. Two other guys got into the car. "Take us up to Andytown, and if you see any road blocks, turn and get the fuck out of it as quickly as possible."

'So we got up into Andersonstown and went into the back of Shaws Road. I didn't know it then, but there was a post office there and they intended to rob it. We turned into the back of the flats that the post office was facing, but the place was covered with army. Someone had gone before them and robbed the place! And the army and the police were all over the fuckin' show. Panic stations then.

'I had to take them back into Ballymurphy and the funny thing about it was, your man in the back who was holding the gun to me turned round and said, "How much do I owe you?" and threw me a ten pound note! Then they all bailed out and went down the entries again at the back of the houses.'

One consequence of the violence – even when it was not clear that the Troubles would last – was that news reporters and their crews flooded the city, determined to report on what was happening. Their arrival meant a dependable new revenue stream for taxi drivers, if the drivers were prepared to take the media where they needed to go.

'My brother started working with the press through pure fluke,' Charlie told me. 'He had met a woman who had started a job with RTÉ as a secretary, and obviously RTÉ didn't want to bring their own vehicles up from the south; they were southern registration cars, and everything was getting burnt and hijacked at that time, so my brother ended up working with them.

'I started doing the same about two or three years later, whenever things had gotten really hot and heavy around about 1972–73. RTÉ would call my brother personally, or me. If it happened that he had two crews coming in on the one day I would have covered for him, and we just worked it between ourselves.'

Working intermittently with the Irish press opened Charlie's and his brother's eyes to the potential profits that could be gained from taxiing the media exclusively. The average customer in Belfast wants either to travel to work, to the city centre to shop, or to visit friends: the average fare, therefore, does not depart the city limits. With Belfast International Airport a rewarding eighteen miles outside Belfast, taxiing the press meant regular runs to the airport and back, and to Derry, Dublin or further south to follow the news as it happened. Charlie and his brother began to take their new side-project seriously, and set about advertising their services.

'We thought about putting an ad in the paper. But I said "No, that's stupid. Who'd read it? We need to try to get camera crews in from abroad."

'My older brother had started dabbling with sound recorders and ended up on the staff of RTÉ. Again, by pure fluke, he met a guy who worked for ITN. We asked him to put up a poster advertising transport, sound and lighting equipment for hire in Belfast on the noticeboard in the ITN building in London and it snowballed from there. The thing just went crazy.

'At one particular stage I must have been working for about twenty camera crews. They would have rang a couple of days before – I'll be over on Wednesday or Friday or whatever. Basically, you asked them what they needed. If they needed equipment you would have hired it, if we hadn't got it already, and you would have gone everywhere in Northern Ireland, depending on what had happened the night before.'

While other private-hire cabbies relied on their employers to keep the meter ticking over, for Charlie, who was his own boss, business was booming, and soon the money began to roll in.

'We made a very good living out of it, very good. Before the press got into the electronic stuff – which now only takes 3.5 seconds to beam from Belfast to Dublin – it was the old reel-to-reel film that you had to bring down to the RTÉ studios in Dublin so that they could process it. I had to do the run down to Donnybrook in Dublin fairly regularly, and I was getting £100 a run.

'I've seen us getting called three times in a single day. That was six times up and down the road, through every wee town and village, with the film and the cameraman, the sound man and the lighting man in the back seat. And the crew would say, "Wake us up when you get to Dublin!"

'As I say, everything was going haywire at that time. After Bloody Sunday in Derry [30 January 1972], it was a couple of weeks later and there was a civil rights march in Newry and the press thought it was going to be a similar sort of incident. So RTÉ decided to try and get the film down to process it as soon as possible.

'They hired two speedboats, had a car on the southern side of the border and a car on the northern side, and they chartered a helicopter from Irish Helicopters, from Haughey, the future prime minister. But in the end the whole thing was a complete flop, nothing happened, and they ended up spending two fortunes just to get the film out!'

The demand from the world's press for Belfast-based taxi drivers who knew the city well, and who were fit and able to cope with the rigours of driving directly into the front line, was overwhelming. As a result, Charlie and his brother were able to provide work for other drivers, mainly from Enterprise Taxis, a firm with which they were both well acquainted.

'We used guys that we would have classed as friends to work with us on a regular basis,' Charlie added. 'We were on twenty-four-hour standby, because anything could crop up at any time of the day or night. If the phone rang and it was three in the morning, or five in the morning, you knew some poor crater had lost their life – they'd found a body somewhere. We went and lifted the crew from whichever hotel they were staying in and away we went. My brother and I stuck to our own press crews, and let the other drivers do what they wanted with the rest.'

As the 1970s wore on and the Troubles escalated, the attention of the world's press became fixed on Belfast. 'Because,' as Charlie admits, 'bad news sells papers.' Having developed a reputation as a reliable driver, Charlie found himself taxiing reporters from every continent to all quarters of the city. Though he admits that some nationalities were easier to work with than others.

'We were working with RTÉ then, but also CNN, NBC, Dutch television, French television, the Chinese, everyone. The Americans, I had a couple of them in my time. They just went completely overboard; everything was done on a big scale. They had to hire a van to bring their equipment in from the airport!

'They used a lightweight case padded on the inside for their cameras, and then they had their film stock. It had to go into a separate case, which was fireproof and all this nonsense. You have no idea the money that was involved. They were okay, but, you know, if you were working with local reporters they knew the scene. They knew not to go too far, but the Yanks just went in hell for leather, straight into the middle of the trouble. There was an awful lot of them got hurt because of the rioting and what have you, but it was through stupidity. If they had watched what the other crews were doing – who knew how to 'do a riot', as they called it – and stood well back, they would have been all right.

'The press chopped and changed. You would have got a well-established reporter working for UTV, and then they would change their mind – through boredom or whatever – and move to another country or go across the water. We met different crews all the time.'

One well-known reporter that Charlie had occasion to work alongside was the famed British war correspondent, Kate Adie, and her Irish equivalent, the equally courageous Olivia O'Leary.

'Kate Adie was with the BBC and Olivia O'Leary was with RTÉ,' Charlie recalled. 'Kate's a very, very nice woman; I met her on several occasions. I don't know how her and Olivia met but they were great friends; they were always joking and carrying on. If anything was happening they always seemed to meet up, and the craic between them was very good.

'There were two incidents I remember with Kate and Olivia. One was in Cromac Street just across the road from Telephone House. The army technical officers had just arrived because paramilitaries had hijacked a post office van and put a bomb in it. There were other cars parked in the square and Kate and Olivia, they were sort of kneeling down behind a car.

'The army officers were getting their gear out and putting their flak jackets on, and Kate and Olivia were arguing with each other, which was common. One would say, "I bet you a pound there's nothing in it." The other would say, "I bet you a fiver there is." That sort of thing.

'So we were all kneeling down behind these parked cars, chatting away and Kate says, "Ah, there's definitely nothing in it, it would have went off at this stage." Then bang! The van disintegrated. The fuckin' thing shot up Victoria Street!

'The following week the two of them met up again and this time it was in Royal Avenue and the van that was hijacked was a *Belfast Telegraph* van and it was parked outside the Co-op building. The Co-op used to be a fairly big store and again, there they were arguing away. "Ah, there's nothing in it." And I said, "Remember Cromac Street!" And one of them said, "You're talking a load of nonsense; there's definitely nothing in it. Sure we've been here for three quarters of an hour." And it just opened up like a tin of beans! The engine completely disintegrated and the axle flew up York Street. The whole bloody thing came down around us. We had to run like hell to get out of the shrapnel with our arms around our heads, but that was standard procedure when a bomb went off.'

Certainly there were very many drivers who would not have cared for such a high-risk job, and worked the communities hoping for as little upset as possible. But for drivers like Charlie, such hair-raising incidents were par for the course.

'There wasn't much point in working for the media if you didn't go into the front line. You took it as second nature. You got a wee bit complacent at times, because it was going on day and daily. In the middle of the riots and stuff like that you'd get battered now and again with the odd brick, stones being thrown. But normally rioters or paramilitaries didn't bother with the media. Normally the media just drove through riots, no bother.

'The media had carte blanche, sort of. There was no messing about or hijacking their cars, bar one incident in Derry that I remember. Even if something happened and you didn't see it, the kids would say, "Mister, mister come on over till you see this!" They would have shown you rubber bullets or plastic bullets lying around. "Do you want one of them? Have you got one of them?" Kids had them as trophies.'

★

Working alongside the press was not all riots and shootings, however, as Charlie confirms. 'We would have met up with different crews three or four times in the one day, so you got to know all the cameramen and the sound guys quite well. They were all good craic. And once they had finished for the day the majority of them used to stay in the Wellington Park or the Europa Hotel – the two main hotels in Belfast at the time. It was a boozing session, all right. The media have always enjoyed their alcohol. I suppose it was to get rid of the tension.'

In time Charlie became accustomed to working in a warzone. Having grown up in Belfast he knew which areas were nationalist and which were unionist, where the flash points existed, where trouble was likely to occur, and which routes to take to get the cameras there fast.

'If there was nothing happening and it was quiet, the crew would have got into the taxi and we would tour around here, there and everywhere, what we used to call 'patrolling'. One day we were on the Glen Road in west Belfast; I think it was shortly after 3 p.m., and we heard a bang. I could see a plume of smoke at the junction of the Glen Road and Shaws Road.

'So we got there and there was a police Land Rover sitting behind this lorry. The policeman, well, we found out later he was dead. Paramilitaries had hijacked a lorry – a parcel van with a load of parcels in the back. The back door was open and two of the policemen got in to see if there was anything suspicious in the back. This sergeant said to the other two, "Don't go near the front of the lorry," and one of the guys went to one side and the other went the other side, opened the door and it blew to bits. He was lying dead and the other guy was seriously injured. We were less than a quarter of a mile away when it happened.'

Charlie understood what reporters needed and where they needed to be. He was not simply a conduit to a story, he became a part of the crew. Experienced members of the press relied on him to take them to and from the front line as swiftly as possible. 'Greener' reporters often relied on him for their lives. Without any combat zone training, Charlie learned how to survive the dangers of the Troubles – the riots, the bombs, countless bullets to dodge – in his own way.

'It started to become second nature working with the press. You always tried to keep behind the army, because you were trying to see what was actually coming in. There wasn't much point standing behind people when they were the ones throwing stones, because you couldn't see the anger. You couldn't see the petrol bombs being lit and all the rest of it. If you were standing too far away and didn't get anything it wasn't worthwhile putting it on television, it was just scrapped.

'The cameramen carried stock and film at the start of the Troubles, when the press used "the Bag", as they called it. It was a black changing bag with two sleeves in it. You'd put your film into it, then you had to take the film out of the can, unwrap it in paper to keep the light from getting into it, change the spool and put it into the tin. That took a while to do, so you were watching out to see it was safe. If it wasn't, you backed off, you got well out of the way.

'The standard procedure, when you were working with a crew, was that you always stuck with the cameraman. Basically, if you were in a riot situation, you were watching out for danger, looking out for the cameraman. You always put your right hand on his left shoulder and, if he needed to withdraw, you were looking around for him, covering his back, because he was only able to look through one eye. If you wanted him to come back you'd just put pressure on his shoulder and steer him back, so that he wouldn't trip over anything.'

Frequently the press gang sought to train their cameras on stories occurring outside of the capital, and in his capacity as the wheels – as well as, so often, the eyes and the ears – of the operation, Charlie drove to other towns and cities.

Derry, Northern Ireland's second city, was quite often

the destination. Largely a Catholic, nationalist city, where Protestants are in the minority, Derry was the scene of several major confrontations between nationalist rioters and the RUC and British Army during the Troubles (including Bloody Sunday in 1972).

'When there was nothing happening in and around Belfast or elsewhere we used to head to Derry,' Charlie remembered. 'All the media congregated in a street called Rossville Street in the Bogside, where Free Derry Corner is. They all used to meet there. There was waste ground on William Street where they parked their vehicles and nobody ever touched them. 3 p.m. was riot time, when the schools let out. As soon as the kids came out of school there was trouble. All the kids started on the army. It didn't matter if they were on foot patrol or in armoured cars, they'd throw bricks, bottles, anything.

'There was one particular incident in summer I remember. There was an army foot patrol on both sides of the street. Of course they were hugging the wall of the Rossville Street flats, on the left-hand side. I just happened to look up at the roof of the flats, because they were throwing stones off the roof, and there's two guys with a full-sized bath sitting dangling over the edge. A fuckin' bath! And when the foot patrol walked under they let it go and it hit your man on the head. Lucky they didn't kill him, very lucky. I don't know how the hell they did it.

'An hour after that things had calmed down a wee bit because it was getting near tea time and the kids were hungry, so they started to filter away. We were standing talking at the corner and there was a reporter that I got to know, an English guy. He was over here for about a year, but then they brought him back to England. He had been away for about six months. We were standing talking. "When did you get back?" I asked. "Oh, we're only off the ferry from Larne and came straight here." I said, "What are youse driving?" "A Granada. It's up the road there." "Where?" "Our driver, he's English, he didn't know how to get around here so we just give him a rough idea and he parked at the top of Rossville Street."

'I said, "You don't park there, definitely don't park there." "Oh, it'll be all right, it'll be all right." This was a brand new Granada with delivery mileage on it and the next thing, half an hour later, it came rolling down the hill, nobody in it, the boot bouncing up and down. They had put a couple of gas cylinders in the boot and, of course, when it hit the wall at the bottom it stopped and the army scattered, thought it was a bomb. It must have been about 8 p.m. that night in summer. The army bomb disposal arrived and blew the feckin' car up and your man got the sack. Obviously the driver didn't know he shouldn't have left the car where he left it. It was his first time in Derry, but it cost him his job.'

Charlie admits that working with the press had its thrills. He looks back fondly on 'the buzz' of taxiing well-known reporters around the country, of helping them find and capture the story of the day, and of watching reports that he played a vital role in recording on the national news in the evenings. He was friends with or had come into contact with several drivers who were not as lucky as him to have survived the Troubles, and is quick to pay his respects to the deceased and their families. But he is grateful that he lived to tell his tale, even if memories of the dark times remain achingly fresh in his mind.

'There's things that you want to put out of your head, to be truthful,' he said. 'One day, in the mid-1970s, we went up onto Black Mountain in Ligoniel. A body had been found in the back of the car, lying across the back seat. The army blew the handle off the car and you could see the two feet dangling out. They put the robot in and the robot put a rope around the feet and they dragged the body out. The guy, his head hit the ground and I'll never forget until it the day I die, there was about an inch of flesh holding his head on. You know, its things like that you don't want to remember.'

But it was the progress of technology rather than the horrors of the job that eventually convinced Charlie to leave his press days behind him. 'I stopped working with the media when the electronic camera equipment came in, when the press started getting their own crew cars and stuff like that,' he confirmed. 'Obviously they were pouring money into covering Northern Ireland hand over fist; anything the media wanted, anything they needed, they got. They weren't calling us anymore; they were driving around in Audis, Jags, top of the range Volvos, anything with speed. And in the 1990s the political parties had started to talk, so the media only congregated at press conferences at Stormont, the Culloden Hotel or at Hillsborough Castle. Things started to calm down and that was it. What happened then was the sound guy was usually nominated as driver, so the work all just fizzled out.

'I still have friends in the press, and my young nephew has his own production company up at Stormont, which keeps us abreast of things. But you don't get the buzz now that you got then. You were just continually going from one incident to the other. You never thought about it, you just bobbed along and when you got out you knew the set up and what to do.

'Before my retirement I worked as a dispatch clerk and day shift manager – I took all the crap that came off them phones and the complaints. But I was glad; I wasn't stuck in the middle of things any more. I was too long in the tooth for that. I started in there shortly after 6 a.m. and finished at 2 p.m. The rest of the day was my own. No weekend work, so it was handy.

'I enjoyed working dispatch. It kept me going and the guys in there were not just workers, they were more like family, you know. If one of our drivers broke down or something went wrong with his car, he could be anywhere in Northern Ireland, but you didn't think twice. You went and got him, and that was it. We were family.'

The Falls and the Shankill Taxi Associations

> In the early seventies, there wasn't the disposable income in Belfast that there is now, and there wasn't the car ownership per household that there is now. People had a heavy reliance on public transport.
>
> STEPHEN LONG
> *former general manager for the*
> *West Belfast Taxi Association*

During the Troubles, although the private-hire sector managed to keep its head above water, many people still relied on public transport as an affordable way of getting in and out of town. However frequent riots on Belfast's streets meant that bus services were sometimes interrupted. Rioters attempting to stop the RUC and the army entering certain areas of Belfast would often hijack buses, set them alight and use them as barricades to block off roads.

By 1969 the Belfast Corporation Transport Department – which oversaw the provision of bus services in the city up to 1973 – had lost several of its vehicles to rioters across the city and, in an attempt to protect its drivers and its buses, decided to suspend certain routes in west and north Belfast. These suspensions occurred intermittently for years, and would have a lasting effect on the taxi industry in the west of the city, ultimately leading to the founding of the West Belfast Taxi Association (WBTA).

With public transport unavailable, west Belfast community groups in the nationalist Falls Road area began to advocate what they called a 'good neighbour policy'. This policy – promoted through pamphlets and newsletters – encouraged individuals to use their own cars to transport passengers into the city centre for a nominal fee.

'In the early seventies, there wasn't the disposable income in Belfast that there is now, there weren't the employment opportunities that there are now, and there wasn't the car ownership per household that there is now,' explained Stephen Long, general manager of the WBTA from 2003–2010. 'People had a heavy reliance on public transport … so someone in the community who had a vehicle would take groups of people into town to go to their work (if they were lucky enough to have a job), or to go shopping, or – in a lot of instances – to go to the post office and collect their benefits.'

Soon the 'good neighbour' group – affectionately dubbed the 'People's Taxis' – began to gather momentum. Many public-hire drivers, who had previously worked the centre of town, saw the benefit of this service and joined; a fleet of black hackney cabs, many of which were well past their sell-by dates, was imported from London to replace the private cars; affordable, fixed rate fares were established (ten pence per adult and five pence for children and pensioners, no matter the length of the journey); and routes were set, from the association's unofficial rank on Castle Street to areas such as Lenadoon, Glen Road and Whiterock.

Although drivers did not deviate from these routes, the cabs could be hailed by prospective passengers at any point between Castle Street and the cabs' final destination. Drivers simply pulled over for whoever happened to wave them down, if there was room in the taxi, and passengers indicated that they wanted to disembark by knocking on the glass partition that separated them from the driver. Large signs were displayed in the front windows of all cabs to let potential passengers know where that taxi was heading.

Passengers could expect to share their cab with other members of the public, who would jump in or out at any point, and in that way the system was similar to a community bus service. You would find an elderly lady with her shopping bags sitting beside two young men on their way to play football; or perhaps a group of women on their way to work, none of whom would have known each other. It is a system that has not changed in the decades that have since passed.

In 1973, with the appointment of a leadership committee, the Falls Taxis Association – which in 1982 became the West Belfast Taxi Association – was born.

'The association was officially formed in a place called Georgie's Shop, which was at the bottom of Beechview Park at the Falls Road junction,' continued Stephen. 'Georgie was synonymous with west Belfast at the time. He opened his shop around about eight o'clock in the evening and kept it open all night, so it was a focal point; known throughout Belfast as somewhere where you could get a cheap packet of cigarettes or a famous cheese bap.'

Georgie's Shop was a place to congregate, to strategise and, in quieter times, a place to debate just who could claim the mantle of first member of the group.

'There is a lot of claim and counterclaim amongst individuals about who was the first person to drive for the association informally,' explained Stephen. 'Another "Who Shot JFK?" job – it'll be disputed forever and a day. But there is one particular person who claims that he was the first unofficial FTA driver. Robert Connelly is his name, but he's better known as Bobby Bus Stop, because he would come down the road in his car, stop at the bus stop and tell people there were no buses on. That nickname has stuck till this day.'

Much like Belfast's sedan-chair porters of the eighteenth

and nineteenth centuries, the FTA – or 'the black taxis' as people usually called them – had carved out a niche for themselves as a public-hire taxi service unlike any other in the UK or Ireland, an independent service which would operate under sometimes terrifying conditions.

Seamie Rice began taxiing for the FTA in the mid-1970s and he remembered, with a wince, attempting to transport passengers amid the mayhem of the riots, which were often sparked, as he said, by army incursions into nationalist areas.

'When an army foot patrol came up the street to lift somebody or raid the houses, trouble erupted just like that,' said Seamie. 'And once the rioting started that was it, everywhere was sealed off. Cars got hijacked and burned; everything was blazing. On these roads you had to drive around burning lorries, down side streets. You were driving over the rubble. You never stopped.

'I remember driving up the Falls Road in the old black taxis with the BMC [British Motor Corporation] engines – all these manual gearboxes. You put your foot on the brakes and the motor was all over the place! I was actually scared of driving those old black taxis, but after a while I started getting used to it,' he laughed.

The FTA kept their services running during the most disruptive of riots and, because of this, commuters on the Falls Road and its neighbouring boroughs – including Poleglass, Twinbrook, Whiterock, Andersonstown and the Glen Road – came to rely on the FTA as the only reliable means of motorised transport into the city centre. The people respected their industry; they knew the drivers, they trusted them, and they gave the association their full support. The FTA had quickly and effectively filled the void that the buses had left.

When it was established, the FTA was an ad hoc and chaotic outfit, but it was based on a firm socialist ethic espoused by its founding members: it was to be run by the people, for the people. The FTA aimed not only to provide an affordable means of transportation, but also to provide employment for the people of west Belfast, some of whom would have struggled to find employment elsewhere. As Stephen Long explained, many of those employed by the FTA were Catholics who had previously been interned by the British government for suspected paramilitary involvement.

'Those who had been to prison for various reasons – republican ideals and everything else – couldn't find employment outside of their areas because of their backgrounds. Here was a means to earn a living for their families and themselves.'

While Stephen acknowledged that the drivers may have been almost exclusively Catholic, he insisted that the FTA services were not restricted to the Catholic community; that FTA drivers did not and would not refuse a fare on the grounds of religious persuasion. Only fares that drivers deemed to be potentially unruly or known troublemakers were refused the service.

'What you have to understand is that the FTA knew there were people from different communities using the service, because all of their routes passed by the Royal Victoria Hospital,' Stephen explained. 'There would have been people of all different religious persuasions who worked in the Royal or who had to visit the hospital – outpatients or family members – so there was never any distinction made between who used the service. It was a very egalitarian, economic way of getting from A to B.'

That being said, no one associated with the FTA will contest the fact that the organisation has always been closely linked to the republican movement in Belfast. Due to this political affiliation, and given that its drivers were mostly ex-prisoners, the FTA often felt that its drivers were being singled out by the army and police for 'special' treatment. Although all civilians who passed through the ring of steel checkpoints were potentially subject to random searches by soldiers and members of the RUC, Seamie contends that FTA drivers experienced more scarches than most.

'The cops and the army, they gave you a really hard time on a regular basis,' he explained. 'Not all the taxi drivers got it, but anybody who was an ex-prisoner did. I was an ex-prisoner myself – I was actually interned in Long Kesh [the Maze Prison] for two and half years from 1971 – so I got a wee turn of it now and again.

'The Brits used to have a clatter of photos on who to stop and who not to stop. They got to know your taxi number, who you were and what you were doing. They'd trail you out of the taxi and make an eejit of you in front of a crowd, start searching you and asking you the stupidest questions in the world.

'This used to happen two or three times a week, maybe more. It depended on who you got on the road. There were specific cops who you just knew would give you a hard time. You had to accept it. I just laughed at them.'

It is perhaps not surprising then that FTA passengers were often considered suspicious by extension. Even if this suspicion was very occasionally justified, Seamie felt that the police were far too quick to think the worst of all the passengers: 'The Brits caught a girl in the motor one time carrying guns and everybody was hoked out, including a nun, would you believe!' he said, shaking his head with disgust. 'The nun was put against the flipping taxi and searched. It was laughable at the time, but as far as the RUC were concerned everybody in the motor was involved.

'They lifted the girl who had the guns. I was only a driver in a taxi – I didn't know who she was – so I got released, but the girl eventually did the rap, about a year. People nowadays take the police to court and sue them for anything at all, but in them days you didn't because they got away with it. They could have lifted you anytime, anywhere. But they gave any ex-prisoner a hard time in them days because they knew what some drivers were up to.'

And, although most FTA drivers were only too happy to

live the quiet life during the Troubles – clock in, clock out, go home, stay safe – certainly others felt an affinity with the republican movement and actively took part in paramilitary operations. In other words, they were 'up to' quite a lot. Some would ferry republican paramilitary volunteers from safe house to safe house; help volunteers in moving arms and explosives from place to place; they would refuse to co-operate with police during searches; or permit a balaclava-clad gunman to borrow their vehicle for a time (mostly, they got their cabs back in one piece).

This cooperation with the IRA was alluded to on more than one occasion during interviews with drivers associated with the WBTA, but when asked to go into more specific detail, few were forthcoming.

'There was never anything knowingly told to us,' said former WBTA general manager Jim Neeson, referring to any direct communications with the IRA. 'We lost a couple of taxis – invariably it was somebody's taxi that wasn't going that well and they wanted to get rid of it. One particular time the IRA put a taxi in the wee entry at Thompson's Garage, full of gear, and blew the bollocks out of the place.'

The end result of this association with republicanism was that the British government and security forces initially looked upon the FTA as an organisation directly involved with the IRA, and because of this, the Department of the Environment refused to recognise the association as a legitimate transport organisation. FTA drivers were refused official PSV licences, and insurance companies declined to do business with the FTA management.

Despite these setbacks, the FTA was still considered a success and, in the early 1970s, in an attempt to mirror that success, a similar public-hire taxi-bus outfit, the Shankill Taxi Association (STA), was established on the staunchly loyalist

Shankill Road – which runs parallel to the Falls – to serve the Protestant community in the west of the city.

'It had to do with public transport,' said Willie, an STA driver. 'In the 1970s and 1980s, with the bomb scares etcetera, the buses weren't running on a regular basis. So people used our taxis, and we had good support.'

The STA established an unofficial rank on North Street – which becomes Peters Hill and then the Shankill Road – in the Millfield area of central Belfast, though, like the service offered by the FTA, drivers did not deviate from their prescribed routes and passengers could hail a taxi from anywhere on the route.

'It worked the same way as the FTA,' added Willie, 'although they went further – up the Falls, towards Lisburn type of thing when the Twinbrook, Poleglass and Ardoyne estates were built.'

The STA was a less ambitious outfit, employing far fewer drivers than the FTA and running only three main routes – North Street to Ballygomartin via the Shankill Road, Bridge Street to Rathcoole, and Bridge Street to Jordanstown. However, it was no less controversial. The STA reputedly had links with the UVF. And during the mid-1970s, the STA employed William Moore, one of the Shankill Butchers. Led by Lenny Murphy, the Shankill Butchers were an ultra-violent loyalist murder gang – the most prolific serial killers in British legal history. Moore, one of Murphy's sergeants, drove the gang around Belfast to look for potential victims in the same cab that he used in his capacity as an STA driver. These connections seriously damaged the reputation of the STA, especially in the Catholic community.

By 1982, however, the success of the FTA was wavering. Now known as the West Belfast Taxi Association it had established an official headquarters in the Conway Mill complex on the

Falls Road, an office on the Falls Road opposite Belfast City Cemetery and a garage at Westside service station at the very top of the Falls Road. But, a full decade after its official formation, the association was no closer to being recognised as a legitimate organisation by the insurance companies, the Department of the Environment (DOE) or the British government, all of whom continued to view it with deep suspicion. On top of that, the association was losing money, and so in order to address this, the WBTA decided to hire a dedicated manager.

A former co-owner of a contract business in Belfast, Jim Neeson was brought in to put the books in order. He was blunt in his appraisal of the association as he initially found it.

'It was a republican organisation – a proud republican organisation – and that worked fine,' he explained. 'They had great co-operative ideas way ahead of their time. They had their own workshops, their own filling station and a drinking club for drivers, a shebeen type thing in Beechmount. But there was no management – the committee was voluntary. And they owed a fucking fortune because of this liberation theology they had: they bought parts from the Brits and didn't pay them back; they played the banks and didn't pay them back either. As long as the wee shopkeeper down the street was paid, that was fine.

'I changed things,' Neeson declared, defiantly, 'and I was, in many ways, hated because of it. But it was a hate that I didn't mind because I'd a justification for what I was doing.'

Neeson describes the association then as being 'very ragtag' – very few formal records were kept, and little was ever written down on paper, meaning that the precise number of drivers working for the association was difficult to determine, but at that time there were around three hundred. Not all of these were full-time members – many drivers would work the morning and lend their cab out to 'their cousin or whatever' for the rest of the day, but the operation clearly needed to be streamlined. Jim cut the number of drivers on the books down to a manageable 250, with a further 23 drivers employed to work the Ardoyne route, and laid off several mechanics who had worked in the association's workshops and filling station. As a consequence, the association's books began to even out.

'The fares were 15p or 20p per passenger,' Neeson explained. 'The drivers paid us £20 a week. There was a proportion of that, two-sevenths, that went to the Green Cross, which was a prisoner-orientated organisation. From the other £14 we took maybe £5 for insurance and the rest went to pay people like me and the other staff. Everything after that was the drivers.'

Of course, there have been accusations that the FTA/WBTA funded the IRA directly, but when asked about this, Neeson was measured in his response.

'An American journalist once said to me in a bar, "If you won't admit that you supplied money to buy guns for the IRA, well you eased their situation by helping them in other matters." If that's right, then that's right. Whatever. If you give somebody a present of £10 and they don't necessarily spend it in Boots, it's entirely up to them. But we did not donate money to the IRA: we helped certain individuals. For instance, the black taxis financed Joe Austin and Denis Donaldson to go to Lebanon to try to secure the release of Brian Keenan.'

Sinn Féin councillor Joe Austin, and Denis Donaldson – one of the IRA's chief strategists who, it was later revealed, also operated as an informer for the British government – travelled to Beirut in 1987 in a bid to negotiate the release of Belfast man Brian Keenan. A teacher at the American University in Beirut, Keenan had been kidnapped on 11 April 1986 and was held hostage by the religious fundamentalist group Islamic Jihad. Austin and Donaldson held talks with representatives of the Amal and Hezbollah groups to secure his release, but no resolution was found and Keenan spent a total of four and half years as a hostage before being freed on 24 August 1990.

'We did many things like that,' argued Jim, who is proud of

the WBTA's positive influence in west Belfast and beyond. 'If someone wants to go through the books of the Green Cross, that's entirely up to them.'

Having tackled the financial difficulties facing the WBTA, in 1988 Jim turned his attention to establishing the legitimacy of the association, doing everything in his power to discredit Margaret Thatcher's claim that the WBTA was 'nearly legal'.

Thatcher was obviously alluding to the association's close relationship with the republican movement in Belfast, but also to the fact that the WBTA remained unlicensed. Her comments encouraged Jim to try and obtain an official licence for the association and cement its place as a viable and efficient taxi transport system in the city.

'You can't be "nearly legal",' Jim said. 'It's like pregnancy, you're either pregnant or you're not. But I took that as a compliment. In a sense, Thatcher was recognising that you don't have to rely on the bus service within an urban conurbation. Ours was the perfect system for inner-city estates.

'We made a petition so that they had to recognise us and give us a licence. I went to the DOE and said, "This half a million signatures, where do you want them?" The guy in the civil service said to me, "Five of them will do me." "What am I gonna do with the rest?" "Well, I'll tell you what Jim, I will sign for half a million and give you a written receipt, but between you and me I'm going to put them in the store and they'll be dumped and all that will remain will be the receipt." But we had a signed petition.

'That day we drove forty taxis around City Hall, closed the fucking town down, and managed to get the road service operator's licence. We were officially recognised then.'

This was not the first time that the association had used the tools at its disposal to instigate change. In 1983 it had used its influence and position in the community to get involved in local politics, firmly and publicly allying itself with Sinn Féin. A proportion of the WBTA fleet mobilised to help voters get to the polling stations during the election, ensuring a landslide victory for Sinn Féin's west Belfast representative Alex Maskey, a former WBTA driver who went on to become the first Sinn Féin Lord Mayor of Belfast.

'Alex Maskey was a member of the Republican movement – he was an ex-prisoner – so he automatically came on board as a driver,' remembered Jim. 'But he wasn't a very successful taxi driver, because he was too involved with Sinn Féin. So when he decided to run for councillor, we put our system behind him. We started off with every driver working for two hours taking people to the polls, and then we refined it. We put five taxis into each polling area: that was fifty taxis off the road that day. The other two hundred drivers got a better turn, so they paid £5 each for the guys at the polls and that meant that they got a full day's wage. Everybody was happy.

'We got an awful lot of people to vote for us because of the taxis. Every election day I went around the different areas, to New Lodge, the Lower Falls, Andytown, Twinbrook, and asked, "Does anyone need transport?" Women would say, "Me, her and her are going to vote at St Teresa's at 12 o'clock. Any chance of running us down to the shops?" "No bother." Eventually, when it came to it, they voted Sinn Féin. Do you know why? "Ach, because that wee taxi man was awful good. He ran us down to the shops, great wee lad."

'That's what the taxis did; we helped put Sinn Féin on the map. We did the same thing in Derry, but we did it particularly well in west Belfast and it worked magic. We won many men and many elections for Sinn Féin, because we ran what was probably the best transport system for any political party in the world.'

In spite of these political achievements, a single event on 19 March 1988, commonly referred to as the corporals' killings, will forever be associated with the group.

66

Three days prior, during the funerals of three Provisional IRA volunteers, loyalist paramilitary Michael Stone had opened fire on mourners in Milltown Cemetery and killed three people, one of whom, Caoimhín Mac Brádaigh, was a WBTA member and IRA volunteer. At Mac Brádaigh's funeral on 19 March, a car carrying corporals David Robert Howes (23) and Derek Tony Wood (24) was blocked by a WBTA cab and mobbed by dozens of bystanders, prompting Corporal Wood to brandish a gun and fire a shot in the air. The two corporals were pulled from the car and taken to nearby Casement Park, where they were stripped naked and beaten, before being thrown over a high wall, driven to waste ground and shot dead. The vehicle that transported Howes and Wood to the site of their deaths was a WBTA black hackney cab.

The British Army maintains that Howe and Woods were engaged in routine communications work at the time, but the republican community argue that they were trailing the funeral cortège undercover. Two IRA volunteers, Alex Murphy and Harry Maguire, were convicted of the murders one year later, in 1989, while three other men were convicted of aiding and abetting Murphy and Maguire. Jim Neeson, who was present during the attack, was arrested along with several others and charged with grievous bodily harm, but was acquitted in 1990.

The deaths of the two corporals marked a watershed for the WBTA. The incident received global attention, and caused a furore at home. Those who had argued that the WBTA was a republican organisation that was not to be trusted appeared vindicated. It was the darkest day in the history of the association, and a horror that many would never forget.

'Everyone knows about the killing of the two corporals,' said Stephen Long. 'It was something that regrettably happened. There's no excuse for taking anyone's life. But what had to be remembered was the previous three days' scenario in relation to the attack. I would have no reservations or hesitations in meeting the family members. I could tell them why we were

67

present at Mac Brádaigh's funeral. Whether it would be a comfort to them I don't know. You can't explain the taking of anyone's life. I think it's totally wrong.'

Given the WBTA's affiliation to the republican movement, it might seem surprising that Jim Neeson and his associates often worked closely with their counterparts at the STA during the 1980s and 1990s. Many FTA drivers were unhappy that the FTA dealt with the STA at all, but Jim asserts that any collaboration between the two taxi associations was motivated purely by business.

'I had a meeting with the Shankill Taxis and we got them their insurance,' he explained. 'All the Shankill Taxi men bought their parts from us. That was part of what we were about; the whole idea was about making money regardless. Most of them, in the main, were not particularly bigoted.

'I know William Moore's brother personally. A nicer man you could not meet. He came up to our yard at Conway Mill to buy parts one day and somebody said, "That bastard's not coming in here, he's one of the Shankill Butchers." So I went out and said, "Do you need to talk to me?" He said, "I know what you're going to say – the Shankill Butchers. That's my brother, nothing to do with me, nothing to do with my fuckin' family." He was such a nice guy, a good guy.'

And the same business savvy that Jim showed in his cooperation with the STA would soon lead him to planning bigger things for the WBTA. In 1997, in an effort to improve the reputation of the association, he oversaw the purchase of a lot on King Street from the DOE; a lot that the WBTA had been using as a base for many years without paying rent. His ambition was to move the association out of Conway Mill, and establish a dedicated WBTA depot.

There was a precedent which had inspired him – Neeson had travelled to the Philippines to learn about the jeepneys, a similarly innovative transport system, also born out of conflict. At the end of the Second World War, when American troops were leaving the Philippines, they sold hundreds of surplus jeeps to the Filipinos, who stripped them down and altered them to accommodate more passengers. These jeepneys rapidly emerged as a popular way to re-establish public transportation, which had been virtually destroyed during the war.

'I was in the Philippines twice studying, and they are exactly the same as us,' he said. 'The FTA was born out of the Troubles – their Filipino jeepney system was born out of the Second World War. It was eerie for me, sort of déjà vu. The first time I got into a jeepney in Manila it was like somebody like me had gone there twenty years before, come back to Belfast and said, "Right, this is what we'll do, we'll set this system up."

'When I came back, I remember being at an after-committee drink in the pub and I said, "I think we should build our own place." "Are you fucking mad?" one of the other committee-men said. "Can we have another pint for this gentlemen, please? I think his head's going." But I had it all thought out, that this was what we should do.'

In the early 2000s, thanks to the Belfast based Sheridan Group – a property development and investment company – Jim succeeded in making his vision for the WBTA a reality. The Sheridan Group bought the land on King Street and, investing just over £12 million, announced their plan to build a new all-purpose building containing apartments, retail space, multi-storey parking and a black taxi depot which would operate from the basement.

On 16 May 2003, this new complex – named the Tannery Building after the Williamson Brothers who had established a Tannery there in the 1880s – was formally opened by former Lord Mayor, Alex Maskey

It is an impressive building, and for several years the WBTA operated there from an underground set-up, where black hackney cabs entered from Castle Street above and circled to a halt around the central office and café area below ground, waiting to be assigned their next route. In 2010, the building underwent further renovation, and the waiting area moved to the ground floor. The underground area is now used as a temporary waiting area for returning drivers where they can chat over plastic cups of tea and coffee, reading newspapers, having a laugh and passing the time of day.

Passengers queue at platforms on the floor above, while floor managers pull the strings, directing fares and assigning drivers. It's like a bustling bus depot, but with smaller vehicles. Today passengers pay a flat rate, no matter the length of their journey, whilst the elderly travel for free.

But perhaps the most striking element of the building is a simple black marble plaque attached to a wall by the entrance. The plaque (unveiled by Sinn Féin president Gerry Adams in 2010) is dedicated to the eight WBTA drivers who lost their lives during the Troubles. There were a number of other WBTA drivers who were killed during the Troubles, but as they were not driving for the WBTA at time of their deaths they are not officially commemorated on this plaque.

'The WBTA was seen as an extension of the IRA's mobile wing,' Stephen Long said. 'It was far from that, but people would have thought of association members as legitimate targets. What legitimacy there is in killing people I don't know, but as far as we were concerned, we were a target.

'Our cars were not the most inconspicuous in terms of their size, dimension and colour. It was quite easy, when they were parked at people's houses, to discern who they worked for, and we had eight association members killed in total, from the inception of the Troubles right up until the present day. Some of them were killed actually driving their vehicles on the routes we serviced, and others were killed in their own homes. But suffice it to say, we lost members of the association who we still hold very dear to our hearts.'

'The first driver killed in my time was Harry Muldoon,'

said Jim. Muldoon was shot by the UVF on 31 October 1984 at his home in Mountainview Drive. 'I got word at 12 a.m. or 1 a.m. in the morning that Harry was shot dead. I had to go to the house.'

The last WBTA member killed during the Troubles was 53-year-old Paddy Clarke, who was shot by the UFF on 2 February 1992 in his north Belfast home. Jim remembers the night he received the call.

'In Paddy Clarke's case it was particularly sad. Paddy was a marvellous man and a great family friend of mine. He was an Irish speaker, a brilliant man, but a bit of snob, in his own way. I used to say to him before he went home from the pub, "What are you having for dinner tonight?" "Stew." "What wine are you having with it?" "I'm not quite sure, I may have a Sauvignon Blanc." So brilliantly funny, but so serious with it. But one day his wife Eda, who was a schoolteacher, rang me in the night and said, "Jim, Paddy's fallen in the hall." I said, "Eda, wake him up and tell him to catch himself on and get up to bed." But she said, "He's dead, Jim. They've shot him. They came in here and shot him dead. Could you come over?" That was the saddest duty I ever had.'

Today the WBTA is looking to the future. Not only has it firmly established itself as a bona fide form of public transport in Belfast, but it has also, through its Taxi Trax tour service, capitalised on the lucrative tourist trade, offering tourists guided tours of the Falls and Shankill roads.

And since the 1998 Good Friday Agreement and the brokerage of peace in Northern Ireland, the WBTA has sought to integrate itself into the community even further, working closely with community groups from the Falls Road as well as the Shankill. Its members are adamant that a return to the sectarian violence of old will not take place on their watch.

'Since the year 2000 we have been working very closely

with the DOE, the Department of Regional Development, the Police Service of Northern Ireland and a number of other statutory agencies,' said Stephen. 'We're a member of Belfast City Management with the City Council. We're a member of the Belfast Visitor and Convention Bureau. We're a member of the West Belfast Traders' Forum and other local traders' associations around the area.

'We work with a number of community groups in relation to issues affecting people in the area, from transport needs to suicide awareness – which is affecting a high volume of people in the west and north of the city – drug and solvent abuse, car crime, alcohol abuse and domestic violence. Whatever it is, we're keen to play a role, because we live, work and socialise in the community.'

It's an admirable legacy, but it remains to be seen if the WBTA will continue in the years to come to be as effective as it has been. The bus service, after all, has long since returned to the west of the city, and car ownership has increased since that first driver pulled up to that lonely bus stop. But there will always be a place for the West Belfast Taxi Association in the history of public transport in Belfast.

The future of the Shankill Black Taxi Association is a lot less certain.

'At one stage, in the early 1970s I think, there were about one hundred and fifty drivers at this Millfield taxi rank,' said Andy, who is now one of only twelve drivers employed by the Shankill Black Taxi Association (SBTA), formerly the STA.

'In busy times you would have got people queuing up around the corner – crowds and crowds of people till one o'clock in the morning – taxis both sides of the road waiting to go,' said Andy, surveying North Street. 'This place was bustling. You had Smithfield round the corner, Co-op the other way, pet shops, off licences, pubs, bars, all sorts.

Everybody came home toward the Shankill this direction ...'

But what was once a thriving commercial centre has obviously seen better days. The worn-down shop fronts and decrepit buildings that now characterise the area are sorry symbols of its decline.

'Now the town's all moved away from Millfield,' Andy added. 'Apart from CastleCourt shopping centre, there's nothing here any more. The area is run down. It was all supposed to be getting regenerated; that's why all the shops went empty. But once Victoria Square shopping centre got all the money, that was all knocked on the head, and everything has gone to pieces.'

As footfall has reduced in recent years, so too has the SBTA workforce. Andy feels that, unless new investment in North Street, and Millfield in particular, is forthcoming, the SBTA is likely to disappear completely.

'I don't think the Shankill taxis will ever pick up again, no. It'll probably just fade out, unless they rebuild this side of the town. Then, maybe we could have forty or fifty taxis here again. Five years ago we had twenty-five or thirty drivers here, now there are only twelve. And in the last three or four months there's been only three new drivers started with us.

'So we're not getting people coming in to keep it up, and it's progressively getting worse and worse. Then it becomes a catch-22; the less taxis there are, the less of a service we can provide. So people from the Shankill, even if they're stood on High Street with all their shopping bags, say, "Ah well, I'm not going round to wait. I might not get a taxi." The bus is £1.70 and we're £1, but people won't walk round here for the sake of 70 pence.

'A lot of the fellas working on the Shankill Taxis have been working here most of their lives. I think three or four of them are pensioners, still driving away. But what else are they going to do? There's nothing for them.'

Clearly the SBTA has not enjoyed the same level of success as the WBTA, but what would have contributed to such differing experiences between two such similar enterprises?

Andy surmised that the WBTA had enjoyed comparative growth, and had the best chance of survival, because of 'community support' and a perceived level of legitmacy that he, and many other drivers like him, contest.

'The WBTA get far bigger support from their community, so they do … When the UVF shot loyalist Bobby Moffett on the Shankill, people immediately said that the Shankill taxis belonged to the UVF, "so we'll not be using them anymore".'

Moffett was shot on 28 May 2010, in broad daylight following an incident in which he had challenged a leading UVF member to a fight. His death led many people on the Shankill Road to want the area free of the UVF's influence, and since the SBTA reputedly had links to the UVF, its business suffered as a result.

'We lost a lot of support from the Shankill community,' Andy confirmed. 'People wouldn't use our cabs in protest. After a couple of months … well, it's like anything: if someone is standing in the rain, protest or no protest, they'll get in your cab. But once you lose people, it's very hard to get them back again.

'Also the WBTA is all legitimised now. But,' he added, forcibly, 'at the end of the day, the IRA – or Sinn Féin, whatever you want to call it – still run it, and that's where the money is going. Nobody can tell me any different.

'In working-class areas all over Belfast, when they tell you there's peace – this, that and the other – certainly there is, but there will always be the men in the woolly faces lurking somewhere underneath. Everybody hates it and everybody moans, but nobody really stands up because look what happened the last fella. In that way,' said Andy, 'Belfast will never change.'

Sally Rodgers and Regal Taxis

> The owner of the building just happened to ask
> my mother, 'Sally, do you want a taxi depot?
> There's one sitting there.'
>
> GERARD RODGERS
> *taxi driver*

When discussing the history of the taxi trade in Belfast with
drivers from all quarters (and, therefore, from both sides of
the political divide), Sally Rodgers' name was one that was
frequently mentioned. As Sally was the first female taxi-
company owner in Belfast, this perhaps is not surprising – if
female taxi drivers are a rarity in Belfast, as they surely are in
most towns and cities, then female taxi-company owners are
rarer still.

Owner and operator of Regal Taxis and employer of
around twenty drivers during the Troubles, Sally Rodgers'
achievements are already noteworthy. But that she managed
to do all of this as a blow-in from the country and a mother
of fourteen is remarkable.

In an industry dominated by men, obviously her sex made
her memorable. But it was Sally Rodgers the individual –
the wife, the mother, the life of the party – rather than Sally
Rodgers the trailblazer who was the subject of many drivers'
fond memories.

Old-school cabbies from the Castlereagh area of east Belfast would talk of her charming County Londonderry accent. Others from west Belfast – and those who had travelled from outside of the city limits to work for her during the 1970s and 1980s – would express their respect for her common touch. Sally Rodgers' reputation as a likeable, affable but infinitely capable taxi-company owner transcended politics and religious bias.

Sally sadly died from cancer in 2006 but her son, Gerard, has continued to work as a taxi driver in the city, and he and his wife Geraldine, were eager to tell Sally's story. Geraldine and Gerard met outside Sally's taxi depot on a busy Saturday night in 1975 and got married two years later, so the depot holds a lot of memories for the pair.

'It's by sheer luck that my mother had a chance to open a taxi depot,' Gerard began. 'It wasn't planned. The flat we lived in on Cromac Street was above an old taxi depot, Gloucester Taxis, and the fella who owned it retired. So the owner of the building, Jimmy McGovern, just happened to ask my mother, "Sally, do you want a taxi depot? There's one sitting there." This was in 1975.

'My mother hadn't a clue about taxiing. She wasn't a businesswoman. She was a no-nonsense countrywoman, a housewife. She was born in 1925 and was originally from Portglenone in County Londonderry. She was about fifteen when she came to Belfast for work, in the 1940s, as soon as she left school. She met my father, Derek Rodgers, somewhere along the line – out dancing, I suppose – and the rest, as they say, is history.

'They boarded in a room in Joy Street, but those old rooms were too small, so my mother and father moved up to a big house on the Ormeau Road, just over the bridge facing the park. My dad, he got a licence to open a bookmakers office in Cromac Street. He wasn't wealthy, but when you've got twelve kids to feed, it was a living.

'Then the Troubles came and we moved again, to a three-bedroom maisonette flat above a row of shops on Cromac Street. There was a wee bakery, a chemist and a taxi depot. Our flat was big enough, because my sister, Kathleen, would have been away. Kevin was married, Terry was married, Geraldine was married, Bernie was married. So there was myself, Dermot, Eamon, Siobhan, Nuala, Peter and Philomena to feed – Sean and Deirdre came later.

'We weren't rich – far from it. Irrespective of my father's bookies, we still ran about with holes in our shoes like everybody else, three or four to a bed to keep warm. There were no luxuries for any of us.'

Jimmy's suggestion that Sally take over the struggling taxi depot – which was only a few blocks south east of Belfast's City Hall and the commercial heart of Northern Ireland – is evidence of the positive impression that she made on the people of Cromac Street and the Markets, even so soon after her move to the area.

Jimmy McGovern was a very wealthy local businessman who owned a vast stretch of Cromac Street. It seems likely that he would have had the connections and collateral to reinvent the ailing taxi depot as a more profitable concern, yet instead he asked Sally, who had no business experience at all, whether she would be interested in taking the reins of a business that employed at least ten people. He clearly saw that she had potential.

According to Gerard, the offer certainly came as a surprise to the Rodgers clan, and to no one more than to Sally herself. It was 1975 and Belfast was a troubled city, and Sally was astute enough to know that to take over a business in the centre of Belfast would draw attention to herself and her family.

Only streets away, the Ormeau Road Catholics and Donegall Pass Protestants occasionally fought each other with missiles, petrol bombs and bullets, while across the Albert Bridge – only three hundred yards away from her front door – riots were commonplace between the Catholic people of the Short Strand and the Protestant people of the Beersbridge

Road and neighbouring streets. Perhaps, Sally thought, it might be wiser to decline the offer and focus on keeping the Rodgers family intact.

And yet the idea of running the depot fascinated her. Domesticity was her entire existence – rearing children, keeping house, and tending to her husband – but, evidently, it was not enough. This was a chance for Sally to reinvent and test herself and so, after some personal reflection and advice from her elder sons, she decided to take McGovern up on his offer. Sally got down to work without delay.

'I was in my twenties at the time, and obviously I thought it was a flash in the pan,' admitted Gerard, 'because my mother didn't have any interest in cars. She never had a car in her life. But my brothers, Kevin and Terry, could drive and get their licences and they started the company with her.

'Only one or two drivers stayed on from Gloucester Taxis to work for my ma, but the depot was established. In the end, my brothers went on nights and my mother did the desk. She kept the depot going; she just learned it.'

Gerard's father kept his distance from Sally's new venture. His and Sally's marriage was solid and enduring, and it is clear that Derek was confident that she could make a success of the business.

'When my mother opened the depot, they had to come up with a new name for tax purposes,' Gerard continued. 'One night they were sitting around the table wondering what to call it, and my dad said, "You're smoking Regal cigarettes; why don't you call it Regal?" So my mother named the depot Regal Taxis, but everybody in the Markets knew it as Sally's Taxis.

'Apart from that, my da had no input at all. He was twenty years in the bookies game – he was getting a good living out of it – and I think that my ma felt that he had his own business. This was hers. She always said that the taxi depot was her wee kingdom.'

'She was a fiercely independent woman,' added Geraldine.

'Even though she had all these kids, she used to say, "This is something I'm doing for me." And, being honest with you, in the years that she had the depot she survived on a couple of hours sleep a night. She was always up at 6 a.m., every morning. During the day she cleaned the flat upstairs from top to bottom. Then she went down to the taxi depot and cleaned it out, her and her daughter Nuala. A couple of hours sleep and she was up again. She made sure the family all got their dinner, then went back down to the depot to make sure everything was in order.

'Then it was away to the Hatfield Bar or the Trocadero for a wee drink. She always loved her carry-out too – vodka and coke, and Carlsberg with a chaser – so she brought her carry-out back to the depot later that evening and that was her until everyone got home and it was closing time.

'She worked hard, lived hard, and played hard. In the end it took a terrible toll on her. But you used to look at her and say, "How are you still on your feet? How are you still going?" She established herself and the depot well, and she got a lot of respect from the people of the Markets because of that.'

A sincere and lasting concern for the welfare of the Markets people – and for those from the neighbouring communities – gave Sally an energy that belied her years and meant that she would never become a wealthy businesswoman. Her 'unique style as a depot owner', as Gerard put it, meant that she could never be described as a hard taskmaster. She was neither avaricious nor overly demanding; by all accounts, the running of Regal Taxis was more of a labour of love for her – she worked because she loved it, not just to make money.

'The big depots now, they're all ruthless. That's their business. Sally didn't see it as a business,' Gerard told me. 'Once she opened the depot, she used it as a means to help the community. She only cared about the people, never the money.

'My ma charged far less depot rent than other companies, maybe £10 at the start. She'd have gone into the Markets

Social Club with that week's depot rent and bought drink after drink after drink. Everybody got one. She was very generous with her money.

'If somebody said, "Sally, I need to get to the hospital, such and such is sick, but I've no money," my mother would have given a docket to one of the drivers and said, "That's £2 off your depot rent next week. Take that family to wherever." Anybody who came to the depot with no money, she did exactly the same thing. She was a big softie for hard luck stories. By the end of the week, a driver might have made ten free jobs up the Ormeau Road!

'And she was always very thoughtful,' Gerard continued. 'Any tragedies that happened in the Markets or on the Ormeau Road she'd be the first to send a wreath. Even when she wasn't well, I'd drive her around to many a funeral and she'd pay her respects.

'I remember there was a car accident in Dundalk one time: one person killed and two or three injured; they were family of people in the Markets. The police must have gone to their house and they just didn't know where to turn. My ma sent two taxis to take them to Dundalk so that they could visit the ones who survived in the hospital. It would have been about £25 to Dundalk, but my ma paid the fares. The people did respect that, very much so.'

Her humane approach did not detract from Sally's firm work-ethic, however, and she drew upon the diligence instilled into her during her traditional country upbringing to keep the depot, as well as the family household, running smoothly.

Order was something that Sally worked hard to achieve. She organised her drivers with a precision that put other depot owners to shame. Weekly, without fail, the drunken hordes would congregate, eager to get home to their beds without delay. With a little bit of strategic thinking, Sally made sure that the depot never descended into chaos.

'When the clubs let out on a Friday or Saturday night

you had the west Belfast crowd, the Ormeau Road crowd, the Markets Social crowd, the Lagan Social crowd – I mean you're talking maybe one hundred people standing inside and outside the depot at any one time. My ma would have organised it all,' recalled Gerard with pride.

'When the west Belfast crowd had drink on them, they were a funny crowd, rough and ready. The Markets crowd was just the same. My ma was always scared of them clashing. So what she did was, she got all the long runs away first, four in a taxi at a time – to west Belfast, north Belfast, Ardoyne, Twinbrook and the like – and kept the short runs waiting in the depot. Her attitude was, "If I can get the long runs away first, we'll have a singsong in the back with the rest."

'There were thirty-six pubs in and around the Markets at that time, and the biggest clubs, like the Trocadero, were getting paid two fortunes, but they had no phones. So my ma said to them, "Would you not put a phone in and I can get the drivers round to you at night?" Lo and behold, they got a phone in. That helped calm everything down.'

As the years went by, and the depot's clientele diversified and grew, Sally was not averse to spreading the workload. The depot that she had inherited was far from state of the art – Gerard remembers it as 'a window with a room in the back', as basic as they come – and it was bereft of any effort-saving communication devices. Everything, therefore, was operated the old-fashioned way: in person, by hand and mouth and nod of the head. With such a vast army of children to call upon for assistance, Sally took advantage. The various depot responsibilities were distributed according to the boss's matronly demands.

'When she was doing the desk at night,' said Gerard, 'the drivers all drove up to the depot and my ma would come out onto the street to give them jobs, because there were no radios in them days. Our phones rarely rang. It was all footfall, all depot work. My ma and our Nuala escorted fares to the drivers. "You go to that car, you go to that car."

'I worked in the depot, too – every one of us did something over the years – but as Nuala got older she did the bulk of the work. She was chief floater. When the drivers pulled up, she was able to call the names out: "Them four to Andytown. Them four up the Ormeau Road. Them four to Ardoyne." That was her job and she was very good at it, because she was like my ma: everybody knew Nuala. She would have said to the fares, "Remember, it's not your taxi, it's the driver's taxi." She got respect for that. The drivers always said, "Whatever Nuala says."'

With Nuala helping to organise the fleet, and her sons working hard as drivers, Sally was able to do what she did best: socialise. She was a naturally gregarious, genial person, someone who loved a singsong and a drink, and why not? During the day, she was the matriarch – fourteen children and a husband to look after. The evenings were hers, and she used them wisely.

'At night, Cromac Street was a hive of activity,' Geraldine remembered fondly. 'Sally's was the only thing open after the bars had closed, so there was always a buzz around the depot. You'd have the priest, Father Newbury, and Sally sitting out the back having a yarn … Even the drivers would have sat around talking, having a wee singsong. It was all very informal, and this in the middle of the Troubles. You think to yourself today, "Did that actually happen?" But it was quite normal in Sally's.'

'If you think about it realistically,' Gerard chipped in, 'my mother had had fourteen kids, so it was time for her to enjoy herself, and through the taxi depot she was able to do that. In them days, years ago, you know what it was like – men went to the bar and the women were left at home. Many a time the men would drink or gamble their money in the bookies, but my ma always saw the women right, and very quietly, too. She never did it in an obvious way. Never made a big show of it or let anybody know. She was that type of woman.

'She also sponsored the women's darts team. She couldn't

throw a dart, funnily enough; she just loved watching it. But she thought that women should be able to go out and enjoy themselves. My mother would have been one of the first women to venture into a bar in Belfast. Women had their own lounges in bars – as long as nobody saw them. But my ma helped to break the taboo.'

If Sally was actively feminist during her taxi days, she was also vehemently anti-sectarian. Having been brought up in the country, where the inequalities and prejudices prevalent in urban settings in Northern Ireland were perhaps not so keenly felt, and by parents who were not political, her formative years were not coloured by any great republican influence. She was raised a good Catholic and raised fourteen good Catholics in turn. But she harboured no hatred for her Protestant neighbours and treated every prospective passenger with equal respect and concern.

'Sally and the priest, Father Newbury, were always worried about people wandering through the Markets,' Geraldine added. 'The Troubles were at their height and it was like murder mile. You had the Provies [Provisional IRA] on one side, the Ormeau Road, and the loyalists on the other, Donegall Pass. People who might have been drinking in the Hatfield, or even in city centre bars, walked up to Cromac Street oblivious to the fact that they could have been shot at any time, irrespective of who they were or where they were from. Sally stood outside the depot when there was trouble and wouldn't have let anybody walk up that road. As much as she loved her own community, she knew how dangerous it was.

'She would never have questioned who you were or where you were going. If you were a vulnerable person and you were on your own – or you were walking up the road and you'd no money – it wouldn't have mattered. She wouldn't let anybody walk up the road if there was trouble. She always sent them home in a taxi.'

'On a Saturday night there was usually trouble in the

Markets,' Gerard continued. 'Not on Cromac Street itself, but between the Markets and Donegall Pass. There were crowds coming down the road throwing stones, and crowds going up the road throwing stones, and we were caught in the middle.

'There was one young Protestant lad being chased by a crowd of young Catholic lads one time, and he ran into the depot for help. He didn't know where he was; he was in shock. My ma closed the door, got him settled and went out and chased the crowd away. Her presence was felt. "Oh, we didn't know it was you Sally." You know, all this.

'My ma said to our Kevin, "Take that lad wherever he's going." So Kevin took him straight to his house in Ballybeen in Dundonald. Our Kevin didn't even know where Ballybeen was. In them days, you would never have been out there. But he got him home and a few days later the wee lad or his parents sent a letter to the depot saying thanks very much for your help and generosity and all that. But my ma only did it just because he was a young lad and he was in the wrong place at the wrong time. That was the type of her.'

Sally's concern for all would not have discouraged loyalist paramilitaries from targeting her depot, which was located, after all, within the staunchly nationalist Markets area. The fact that she was Catholic was reason enough for her to be singled out. But Regal Taxis was located on Cromac Street, within the ring of steel, and on the lower Ormeau Road and again on East Bridge Street, the security forces maintained a constant presence at permanent security checkpoints. This made it very difficult for paramilitaries to carry out an attack on the depot, and Gerard was thankful that Regal Taxis managed to survive the Troubles unharmed.

'I can honestly say that the depot was never targeted,' he said. 'My ma never had any security, but there were always plenty of police patrols up and down Cromac Street, because it was a main road. There was a permanent road block near the depot. There weren't that many riots in the Markets, believe it or not, only skirmishes, and I would say that that maybe had an influence.'

As much as she tried, however, Sally could not avoid the Troubles entirely. In the mid-1980s one of her taxis was hijacked by a paramilitary volunteer to be used, as it transpired, as a getaway car in a shooting. Subsequently, Sally found herself in police custody. She was in her late fifties at the time.

'She put a fare into a taxi one night and it was hijacked: they took the car and shot somebody,' Gerard explained. 'Thankfully the person survived, but the driver panicked and told the police that my mother had assigned the fare. That was her job; she put dozens of fares in taxis on that particular night. But the police lifted her anyway.

'She ended up in Castlereagh Police Station for two days trying to explain the situation, and she in her late fifties! The police thought that Sally had set it up – she would have been the last person to see the hijacker. They said to her, "You live in a nationalist area, you must know who it was." But my mother didn't know anything about it.'

In order to protect herself and her family from any sort of paramilitary retribution, Sally gave the police a false description of the hijacker. To do so was common, according to Geraldine. 'It happened to Gerard and other drivers many times,' she explained.

The Markets was a tight-knit community where, Geraldine insisted, 'everyone knew everyone else'. If the police had found out the identity of the shooter, it would not have taken long for the paramilitaries to discover the source of that information. If she had given an accurate description, Sally would have been branded a 'tout', a traitor to the Markets people and the republican cause. The punishment for such a betrayal, as the paramilitaries would have seen it, was death.

'You couldn't tell the truth,' argued Gerard, 'irrespective of whether or not you actually knew the person. Even the police knew you couldn't tell the truth. They knew the score.

So they said, "Look, tell us something and you'll be out in a couple of hours." So she gave them a bum description, the total opposite of what the hijacker looked like. Eventually, they let her go. Nobody ever got charged with the shooting, and the driver never came back to work. He was too frightened. In the end he emigrated.'

'Sally was in a no-win situation,' agreed Geraldine. 'But all the policemen knew Sally, and they respected her. They turned a blind eye to the fact that her depot was open later than it should have been because they knew Sally was doing them a good turn by helping to clear the streets. They knew in their hearts that she wasn't doing anybody any harm.'

Back at the depot, Sally continued to operate Regal Taxis according to her unique philosophy. She was ever-present, the consummate host, waving and chatting with passers-by and inviting everyone to stop off for a gossip. She was someone who understood the value of community and encouraged others to value it too.

Sally created a meeting place within the Markets, a hub, and perhaps that was her ambition from the very beginning. Her depot was compact and elementary – there were no seating booths, no jukebox or slot machines to keep the punters comfortable and entertained – but she had a kettle, a refrigerator and a will to listen and laugh and learn about others. It was not all hard times and trauma. Sally enjoyed her job, and she made many lasting friendships.

Peggy Whyte was one of Sally's closest friends in the depot. She had worked for Father Newbury 'doing chapel work, like a secretary,' said Gerard, but fell into taxiing after Sally offered to take her on as a driver.

'Peggy was a very smart woman,' remembered Gerard. 'She was from the Markets, and she had brains. All of her kids are schoolteachers today or professors at Queen's University, every one of them well educated. And Peggy would have sat in the depot talking to my mother all day. If somebody needed a lift up the road, she'd have run them up. She wasn't getting paid for it, so my ma said, "Do you want to be a driver?" '

'Peggy was very much in the mould of Sally – one of the few female taxi drivers who worked for her – and that's why they got on so well,' Geraldine added. 'There was not a bad bone in either of their bodies. I often used to look at the two of them and think, "Youse are just doing this for the laugh." '

Peggy and her husband Isadore lived with their young family on University Street, close to Queen's University, today an area where students of all nationalities live alongside university professors, young professionals, artists and immigrants, but which in the 1980s was little more than a dividing line between the republican lower Ormeau Road and the loyalist Donegall Pass. It was, at times, a dangerous place to live.

'In 1983 the UVF threw a bomb over the back wall of their house,' recalled Gerard. 'But Peggy wasn't targeted because she was a taxi driver; her family was targeted because they were a Catholic family living on University Street. Your man threw the bomb over their wall, it bounced back off the barbed wire and blew his leg off. He blew his own leg off. But Peggy, being good-natured, went out and put blankets over him, said a few prayers for him. This young fella got ten years suspended sentence. He didn't go to jail.'

Sadly Peggy's compassion for the young man did not stop the UVF from attacking the Whytes' house again: on 12 April 1984, only a year after the first attack, they planted a time bomb on the windowsill at the front of the Whytes' house.

'Peggy was killed outside her own front door,' said Gerard. 'My ma didn't last long after that.'

Peggy's death signalled a watershed for Sally. Gerard and Geraldine maintain that she lost her enthusiasm for the depot shortly after and, although she kept control of Regal Taxis for another six years, she vowed to sell up at the first possible opportunity. In 1990, fifteen years after purchasing it on a whim, she sold her beloved taxi depot.

'Looking back, after Peggy died it was almost like Sally didn't want the depot to continue,' Geraldine explained. 'All of a sudden she wanted shot of it, and she didn't even want it to go to any of the sons. She was determined.

'It was her domain and that was that. When it was gone it was gone. It was sold two or three times after that, but nobody made a success of it. These people ran it entirely differently to how Sally ran it. They tried to make a business from something that was like a charity. The drivers wandered back to the west, the north, went back to the black hacks, and that was it. There's no depot there today.'

In the early 2000s, Sally was diagnosed with bowel cancer, and in 2006, at the age of 81, she was admitted for the last time to the City Hospital. She was diabetic, and had suffered a collapsed lung some years previous.

'She was in hospital, terminally ill and on morphine,' remembered Geraldine. 'She hadn't smoked in twelve years, hadn't drank in ten: her lung had collapsed and she had had to give them up. But, suddenly she woke up and wanted to go to the Hatfield; she said she wanted a cigarette and a drink. So we said, "Aye, you can go. Another week, give yourself a week,"' said Gerard. 'But she died within two days. On the day of her funeral, the chapel at St Malachy's – a big chapel on Alfred Street – was literally packed to the rafters. You couldn't get moving inside. It was the first time I'd ever seen the upstairs being opened for a funeral to let the people in to sit down.' He shook his head, disbelieving. 'But it wasn't really a sad affair. People were telling stories about my mother to the priest, who had come over from America for the funeral, and they had the whole place enraptured.'

Sally was buried in Milltown Cemetery, and left fourteen children and sixteen grandchildren behind her. Her husband Derek died two years after her, on 12 May 2008.

There is little doubt that Sally Rodgers was a pioneer within the taxi industry in Belfast. There have been female company owners since – and many female drivers – but it is her story that continues to inspire. As a countrywoman she did not let the big city daunt her. As a mother of many, she did not let her household decline nor her family split. As a businesswoman, she led by example, and worked only to keep her employees in jobs and her doors open. More than twenty years after Sally consigned Regal Taxis to history, it remains alive and well in the memories of so many taxi drivers in Belfast.

But it is to those who knew her best that the final word should be left.

'The people of the Markets loved her because Sally was just Sally,' said Geraldine. 'She knew her own mind and she was a woman of her time. Even today, all the drivers speak well of her: she had a great rapport with them. She was so approachable, and she definitely didn't do it for the money. Sally was the worst taxi woman, moneywise, ever.'

'Every taxi driver in Belfast knows about her, because at one point in time – throughout the whole Troubles, even if they weren't legit, if they were down on their luck and needed a job for a week or two weeks – they all went to Sally's. She was a one-off taxi owner,' Gerard concluded. 'Nobody could replace her.'

Working in a Man's World

I think the men probably found it as difficult as I did when I started, because I was a woman coming into a very male-dominated environment. It was like they were more scared of me than I was of them!

MAJELLA MCKEOWN
driver for West Belfast Taxi Association

Although most private-hire companies in Belfast have at least one female driver on their books at any given time, women taxi drivers are a rarity in Belfast. A glance at the middle-aged male faces that congregate at any of the public-hire ranks in the city will show you that female black cab drivers – public-hire drivers – are rarer still. Taxiing is traditionally a male-dominiated profession, and there are many reasons why women tend to gravitate towards other lines of work.

Taxiing has inherent dangers and drawbacks which men, it is generally assumed, are more capable of handling: the long, unsociable hours; the armies of inebriated fares that come with the night shift; long periods spent alone at ranks, waiting for customers. The list goes on. But the female taxi drivers I met were not only pleasant and polite, but were potentially more capable of dealing with problematic situations – like changing a tyre, or locating a particularly hard-to-find street

– than some of the male drivers I have met.

I was lucky to have been introduced to two female drivers, Deirdre Welsh and Majella McKeown, who, on the face of it, seemed quite alike: both are in their early fifties, share similar upbringings and have been driving for some years now. But their experiences of driving taxis are very different.

Deirdre is not married and has no children, is employed in the private-hire sector, works on Friday nights as well as during the day and prefers the professional company of men to women. Majella, on the other hand, is married, is a mother (and grandmother), is employed in the public-hire sector, driving a public-hire taxi-bus for the WBTA. She only ever works the day shift and found it rather more difficult to get used to the male-dominated taxi industry than Deirdre.

Despite their differences, however, both women see their job as a sort of essential public service which many disadvantaged members of the community rely on, and they derive a great deal of job satisfaction from knowing they are playing a positive role in those people's lives. Despite the difficulties they have often come across in their time taxiing in Belfast, it is a job that complements their contrasting lifestyles well.

I met Deirdre one lunchtime in the quiet headquarters of Value Cabs, the private-hire company she works for, and soon learned that she feels more at home amongst men, more comfortable and confident than Majella, because of her previous experience in a similarly male-dominated work environment: before applying for a PSV licence, she was one of only four female street sweepers employed by Belfast City Council.

'I started as a road sweeper during the Troubles, when they had the old tin bins. I was quite young, only twenty-two, and did that for about fourteen years,' Deirdre explained. 'With the council there were a lot of older men, and it was an experience to work with them.

'The council had never had a woman road sweeper before, so they wanted women out on the main roads so that the public could see us. But if one of the men didn't turn in for work I was sent out to clean the entries, or to drive one of the lorries picking up fridges and washing machines. And if the man I was working with was lifting up washing machines, I was expected to lift them too. They used to say, "You're a woman, and you'll do what we do." I really loved that.'

From working exclusively with men, Deirdre next found employment in a field of work that is traditionally populated by females: the cleaning business. It was not to her taste at all.

'I worked for a hygiene company for a couple of years and it was horrible,' Deirdre recalled. 'The money was awful and I was working with a lot of women, and believe me, working with women is far worse than working with men. I had a van. I might have been in Donegal one day, Omagh the next: that was the only good thing about it. But when I got back to the depot the women were always picking at each other, chatting behind backs. I was used to working with men and I found that there was more cattiness amongst other women.'

Discovering the joys of the open road eventually led Deirdre to consider taxiing. 'My brother-in-law worked for Value Cabs and he said to me, "You're not wise. You're driving all day anyway, you should get your taxi licence," and that's exactly what I did.'

When she arrived at Value Cabs Deirdre was prepared for an onslaught of dirty jokes and putdowns, but they were not forthcoming. She was pleasantly surprised. 'The fellas in here are great,' she beamed. 'You get the odd one that moans, but genuinely you get a laugh with them. We have areas outside of the depot where we all meet up, busy areas like Castle Court where drivers queue up next to our free phone, and it's great craic. Somebody will always be winding somebody up.

'It's good banter between the drivers here, because everybody's in the same boat. Value Cabs was only open about a year when I joined – I'm probably the longest serving female driver here – and there are quite a lot of fellas here as long as me. They're the ones you get to know by name.'

For Majella, who worked in catering before coming to taxiing, getting used to working with so many big, boisterous Belfast men took some effort; for her, it was a culture shock.

She disagrees that male taxi drivers are less apt to gossip and bitch behind backs, and even today, after years of taxiing, prefers to keep her distance from those male colleagues she regards as serial grumps. 'I never knew this before,' she began, 'but men are very bitchy. They're far bitchier than women in the workplace, and I found that very difficult to begin with.

'I needed a change of job and I liked driving, so I wanted to try taxiing, and to be honest I think the men probably found it as difficult as I did when I started, because I was a woman coming into a very male-dominated environment. It was like they were more scared of me than I was of them! I found the men to be quite cliquey at the start, but I suppose you get that everywhere, wee cliques and crowds who love a bit of gossip.'

Over the years, however, Majella learned to adapt. 'I just stay out of it,' she explained. 'It's okay now, I've got used to it, really. Now I think the men are dead on; 95 per cent of them are lovely.'

That is how Deirdre and Majella see their male colleagues, but what do their male passengers think of them?

'I've picked up fellas before who have got into the cab and said, "All right mate?"' smiled Deirdre. 'Then they realise what they've said. "Oh, I'm just so used to saying mate, I'm sorry, love." Then they don't open their mouths again because they're so embarrassed. It's hilarious. It's like they sober up there and then, they're too scared to speak. I say, "It's all right, I get that all the time."'

Having a female driver ensures that most fares, whether consciously or otherwise, are on their best behaviour. However, there are those who will take advantage, safe in the knowledge that a woman driver is far less likely to pose a threat or lock up the doors on the way to the police station than a man.

'One night I got called to the Waterfront Hall,' recalled Deirdre, her usual calm replaced by fury. 'They told me that security would let me in. It was only about 8 p.m. on a Friday night, and I thought that the fare must be a disabled person, because we would be allowed to drive right up to the front door for a disabled passenger to get the wheelchair in and all. But when I looked in my mirror I could see two guys helping a woman out who was stocious drunk.

'When they came over they said, "Can you take her home?" I said, "Look, no. I don't think so." She wasn't a nice drunk, you just knew. But the fella said to me, "Well, you're a woman and she's a woman. You wouldn't like us to leave her sitting here, would you?"

'She couldn't even tell me where she was going, so they looked in her bag and found a family allowance book or something with an address on it. So I took her, and from the moment I left the Waterfront Hall until I got her home, she punched and kicked me, bit me, pulled my hair, she even made a pass at me. Everything. Then, when she was getting out of the car, she turned and said, "Fuck off, you're not getting paid." Other male drivers would have lifted her and thrown her out on to the street, but I couldn't. The state she was in, I couldn't even have got her out.

'That was one of the nights when I thought, "I can't do this anymore. When another woman does that to you, that's it." I just knocked off and went home. But there's no point in complaining. You just take it as it comes. I don't know whether I'll ever get a gold watch for service to Value Cabs or not, but I'll still be here, touch wood, in the foreseeable future.'

Majella moved to Belfast from Newry after marrying a man from the west of the city. So, when it came to choosing an outfit to work for, the WBTA seemed like the most sensible option. Majella knew west Belfast well. She was familiar with some of the WBTA drivers, customers and most of the routes. For her, private-hire taxiing was not the way to go.

'The thing I like about the WBTA is the fact that there are so many drivers, two hundred and forty of them in total, and all the drivers look after each other,' she explains. 'You go up and down the Falls Road and there are always two cabs in front of you and two behind, so you're never on your own.

'If you have a passenger causing you a bit of trouble, you've got support and loads of back up, whereas I think with private-hire taxis you're on your own going into housing estates and picking up people at their door. I don't like the sound of that; I don't fancy private-hire at all.

'I've had a couple of teenagers drinking beer and then firing the bottles out the windows and shouting abuse at people before, but all I had to do was stop and ask them to get out and another black taxi pulled up behind me and the driver jumped out to help. This taxi is your office; if anything happens to it you can't work. So I'll be protective over it. I'll tell people, "Don't bang my doors!" But I can rely on the other drivers to be protective for me, because there are enough of them. I couldn't fight myself out of a paper bag!

'There is also a sort of code at the WBTA; we have all these signals. If I go up the Falls Road and there is a driver in front of me and I let him out, then he owes me, so the next pick up is mine. If I see a driver put their hand on the roof of their cab, it means that the next pick up is mine. If I break down and I stop and put my bonnet up, that means I need help, so the next driver coming along will stop.

'I think public-hire is safer for women. It's also very flexible for women with kids who may have parent/teacher meetings and school runs to work around. For example, I don't start early anymore. I take my wee granddaughter to school and then I get the taxi ready – check the oil and the water, clean it and get ready to go for about 10.30 a.m. – and that's me started for the day. It's flexible and I like that.'

When Majella first started taxiing she was assigned to the

night shift. It was a frightening experience, and she has since stopped working nights completely.

'I used to sit outside the pubs and it was okay, but once I went down to the Devenish Hotel about 1.15 a.m., where they were all getting out of the disco, and I didn't even get to the turn-off before they started bouncing all over the taxi, jumping on it and shouting, "Take me, take me!" That scared the life out of me and I didn't do it again.

'Don't get me wrong; in general Belfast is a nice, friendly city. The people are very accommodating. It's just that now, I don't ever work nights or take drunk people. I think that, if I worked nights and people were drunk and being offensive, and sitting in the front seat beside me, I would be scared, so that's why I don't take them.'

Conversely, Deirdre has few objections to working the night shift and believes that working for a private-hire company like Value Cabs, fonaCAB or one of the smaller firms is a safer option for drivers of either gender.

Owned by Stephen McCausland, William John McCausland's grandson, Value Cabs employs over six hundred drivers, and each of their cars is equipped with a security button that links back to the dispatch office and to all other Value Cabs drivers who are on duty. Value Cabs also operates an Interactive Voice Response system (IVR), which ensures that reliable, regular customers take precedence over unknowns.

'Generally the IVR system keeps us safe,' Deirdre confirmed. 'An IVR is a regular customer, a house number or a hotel that uses us constantly. We have all of their details on our system: the phone number, the house number, the address, everything. So if it's an IVR number I'll go into a housing estate without hesitation, because I know – and the girls in the office know – that they're regular customers.'

If dispatch considers a non-IVR number to be safe, nevertheless the driver assigned the fare can refuse the job on his or her own discretion and allow another driver in the vicinity the opportunity to take the job.

Having worked the day shift and the night shift during her twelve years taxiing in Belfast, Deirdre has developed an intimate knowledge of most areas of the city, and close relationships with many of her regular fares. She feels safe to pick up the majority of fares assigned, relying on the checks and balances that are in place at Value Cabs, and sleeps easier because of them. Yet, with experience comes foresight and the ability to spot dangers before they arise and to cope with them effectively when they do.

'Once I pulled into a street and I knew I was either going to be hijacked or robbed,' recounted Deirdre. 'It was a Friday afternoon at Christmas. As I pulled into the court this guy was standing with his hood up holding a mobile phone. I turned and came back again and he watched me. He got on his mobile phone: he must have been warning the ones at the top of the street, "That's the taxi coming in now, just get ready." So I knew then; he gave it away. I just drove by him and said, "It's not happening" and drove out.

'A lot of people will say to you, "What's it like, taxiing? Are you not scared at night and all, are you not frightened?" I've taxied loads of different characters over the years, and it can get scary sometimes, but you're not on your own all the time. Once I picked up a man from a well-known restaurant in Belfast. It was the winter and it was getting dark and he was trailing a bag, which I thought really unusual. He said to me, "I have to go to a cemetery." "Do you know where the cemetery is?" I asked. He said, "No, but you just keep driving." I said, "Well, do you know the area of the cemetery?" He said, "No, just head towards Lisburn and then head into the country." Then he started to tell me that he had got divorced from his wife and it had all turned nasty, and I'm looking at him and looking at this bag and thinking, "Where am I going?"

'As we got into Lisburn the conversation got really tense. I kept asking, "Do you know where we're going?" And he said, "No, I told you to just drive." I had the panic button, a security button that we can press at any stage. When you hit that button, it comes up on our data head: "Driver in trouble." And before you know it other drivers are all round you. They'll leave where they are and head in your direction. But I didn't know whether to push it or not.

'So, as we got into Lisburn there was a whole queue of taxis queued up by the side of the road. I pulled up and wound my window down and said to one driver, "Look, this guy is looking for a cemetery and I'm not sure of the area. Is there any chance you can take him?" I think the fella knew by my face that there was something not right, and by then it was too late for the man in the back to do anything about it. I said to him, "This driver is going to take you wherever you need to go, because I'm really not sure of this area." "Oh, all right then. Fine, that's okay." Out he got, and I couldn't stop thinking, "What has he got in that holdall?"'

When she is working, Deirdre is in constant contact with the Value Cabs base and the girls who work in the dispatch office. It is reassuring to know that, at any time she can radio through to hear a familiar voice, raise a concern or ask for information on a particular fare or area.

'The girls in the office that take the calls aren't stupid either,' she stated. 'If they're a bit worried with the voice of a caller, they will radio me and say, "Driver 98, just be careful of that job." At the same time, if I'm wary about going into a housing estate at 4 a.m. in the morning, I can radio through to the girls and say, "Look, I'm not happy about this job."'

Occasionally, however, a dodgy fare will slip through the net. As polite as a fare can seem over the phone, in person they may turn out to be anything but.

'I have never had anybody really bad in my taxi,' said Deirdre, 'because basically the people in Belfast are very kind. The only bad one I had was an American man. He was just rude. He was with his daughter and they had a wee bit of time to spare before I took them to Central Station, so he said to me, "Would you take us on a tour of the city, up the Shankill and down the Falls?"

'As we were driving up the Shankill he turned to his daughter and said, "Do you see what I mean? Second-class citizens. Look at the way they're living. Look at that scum. You wouldn't get that in America." He literally thought that Belfast people were the dirt on his feet.

'I turned down Lanark Way and onto the Falls and it just got worse and worse. In the end his daughter had to stop him. "Right dad, I think you've said enough."

'Now, I'm not supposed to do anything – I'm just supposed to drive – but I was choking to say, "Hold on a wee minute here, I'm one of the people you're talking about. I'm working-class. Do you want me to throw you out in the middle of them and let them know what you're saying about them?" A lot of our drivers would put you out for less: some of them are big fellas. I couldn't get him out of the car quick enough.'

For Majella, dealing with the general public is no different. 'The public can be very, very hard to work for sometimes. They're very critical. Even on Christmas Eve they'll moan and complain, 'Why are there no taxis?' If you're going home and you put your 'Not Working' sign on they stand on the side of the road and shout at you and call you names. If I had a normal job and I was going home nobody would do that to me, you know?

'Then you get smelly people, people with bad odour problems, nut cases who take their shoes off. You can't do anything about the smelly ones. You can open the window and try not to breathe, or breathe up your sleeve until they get out. And they always sit in the front.'

Of course there are other fares that make the job worthwhile for Deirdre and Majella, people they enjoy spending time with, listening to and helping when the opportunity arises; fares who, over time, become comfortable enough in their company to divulge sensitive, personal information and to whom Deirdre and Majella are happy to give advice and assistance. Some fares will only speak frankly – or even speak at all – to female drivers. In this respect, the job can be very different for women drivers.

'We get all sorts of stories every day of the week, and people come to rely on us. I can remember picking a girl up not so long ago,' Deirdre recounted, 'and she said to me, "You'll not even remember this, but you took me to the hospital one day in an awful state." She said, "I'd been raped that day." Then I remembered. She told me at the time that she couldn't even bear to be near her brothers. I've since come to know her like a friend, and she's sort of coming out of it now. She asks for a female driver, and nine times out of ten she'll get me. When you request a female driver it's an extra £5 on your fare, because I could be at the other side of town. But when I get to the destination and she says to me, "What about the extra £5?" I say, "You've had enough trouble without me adding to it, love. So just forget about it."'

For Majella, good deeds – both received and proffered – make the job go more smoothly.

'I got a wee old man when I'd only started a few weeks, he wanted to go to Whiterock and when he got out he said to me, "Thank you for a lovely, safe journey. I almost fell asleep there!" That kind of thing makes your day. It's nice to know that somebody thinks your driving is good and that you're a safe driver. It shows that it wasn't a white-knuckle ride, so that's a compliment.

'There's another man who lives in Twinbrook. He's old, in his eighties, and he knows all of the drivers. He goes into town every day to this wee club and has a drink when he's there, so he always comes out of the town blocked drunk. When I get him I go off route and take him home, straight to his front door, which is beyond the call of duty because you don't get paid any extra for that and he's always really grateful.

'If I see old people standing on the side of the road, waiting for a taxi, I go and help them with their shopping. Old people sometimes get embarrassed because they're taking so long to get in and out of the cab, and it's nice to be able to say to them, "Take your time, you're all right. I've a mummy too; we're all going to get old."'

Such good deeds may not go unnoticed by people in the community, but they tend to go unreported in the press. Majella thinks that good taxi drivers don't always get the respect they deserve, and lays the blame partly at the media's door. 'It's stuff like that that the newspapers don't print,' she remarks. 'They print that we charge people too much, or that there aren't enough of us on the road. You always read bad things about drivers of black taxis, because people don't write in to newspapers about the nice things that we do.'

So, why are there not more female taxi drivers in Belfast? The safety checks are in place. In these harsh economic times, the money is good. Job satisfaction can be very rewarding, and female companionship in the tearoom or at ranks is not entirely nonexistent.

'It's very seldom that you see female drivers in Belfast,' Deirdre confirmed. 'They come and go. You never really get to know them as well as you do the fellas. Now and then you see a female face and you say to one of the other drivers, "What happened to that girl?" "Dunno, she left."

'When I started here, there was me and another girl. We'd have sat at the Hilton Hotel and had a wee yarn, but she left. Whether it was because she had children and family commitments, or couldn't put in the hours, I don't know, but you need to put the hours in to earn money in taxiing and maybe it's not worth their while.

'I work Monday, Tuesday, Wednesday, Thursday, a short day on Friday and then I come in Friday night again and work through to maybe 2 or 3 in the morning. I take Saturday off and work an open shift on Sunday, which means I can come and go, book in at 6 a.m. and go home at 12 p.m. You can't do that with other jobs. I have no children; I'm not married, so I have that freedom. I don't know whether I could do a job where I worked inside all day. I've always been out and about, driving.'

And Majella agrees with Deirdre that many female taxi drivers do not last long in the job.

'There have been a few women drivers who have started at the WBTA in my time and left for different reasons. They just couldn't stick it; some because they had too many problems with their taxis. It's pure luck when you buy one of these black taxis. If you look after them and service them, which is what I do with mine, then you should be all right, but if you have one that has an engine going one week and a gear box the next, you can get fed up with it, and there's been a few women drivers who've had that.

'There was one girl who had a hit and run accident, had a lot of damage done to her taxi, and she had to pay for that herself. Then the taxi was due its annual PSV test [which ensures the vehicle is roadworthy]. Then she had another accident. Nobody's going withstand that. You need to be really organised. If you're off the road or you're broken down, you need to have savings for back up.

'But, with taxiing, if you need money, you can go do more hours. If you have something coming up that you need more money for, then you just go out and earn it. You can't do that with a normal job.

'I'll probably keep driving for another couple of years. It's secure at the minute, one of the most secure jobs you'll get. All right, so January and February are always really quiet months, when it's not busy, but it's like that for everyone.

'In general there's no threat taxiing, whereas other people like joiners, electricians and builders are losing their jobs left, right and centre: people who thought that their jobs were 100 per cent secure. I think taxiing is one of the safest jobs you'll get.

'Saying that, it's not an easy job. It's tiring. You may not

102

think it is, when we're just tootering up and down the road all day, but see when you're concentrating for five or six hours on the trot and watching your mirrors, it can be very tiring, mentally and physically ... You need to have a lot of tolerance for traffic, to like driving and to be fairly easy going in taxiing.

'I've always liked driving; I find it relaxing, until about 5 p.m. and then I start getting ratty when the traffic's really bad. I'm all right for most of the day, usually until I'm nearly going home. Then I know I need to go home. The hands start going. I have no patience at all.

'I have a daughter and I wouldn't encourage her to taxi. I'd prefer that she did something that stretched her brain a wee bit, and paid a lot more.'

Belfast City Airport Taxis

In a way, I'm an ambassador for Belfast – same
as all taxi drivers in the city – and I tell people
that we have a culture here.

JIM DICKSON
driver for Belfast City Airport Taxis

Taxi depot common rooms are much the same across Belfast.
No matter their location, whether in a plush, purpose-built
building or a single-paned, badly painted former store room
above a pizzeria, there are certain conveniences that all good
common rooms share in order to meet the needs of the
drivers who congregate there. There is the obligatory tea and
coffee machine, of course, which sometimes works but often
could do with a service. Usually an old terrestrial television
or radio sits in the corner, surrounded by battered chairs that
have seen better days and wonky tables where drivers can rest
their boots. Nothing needs to be new, just so long as it works.
Fliers, notices and naughty sketches litter the walls, providing
information on fund-raising initiatives, staff dos and the
perceived figures of certain drivers' naked wives, while bikini
calendars – well-thumbed and out of date – are frequently
found tacked to noticeboards.

While many taxi depot common rooms hum with the
chitter chatter of drivers and dispatch workers socialising

during downtime, one such common room in Belfast veritably vibrates with activity. It is not the gang of drivers in attendance – all of them male – that make the place move, though they come and go with rapid frequency at certain times of the day. Rather it is the thirty-tonne, jet-propelled commercial airliners barrelling in overhead to land at George Best Belfast City Airport, where this particular common room is located.

The airport's single runway welcomes incoming traffic just a couple of hundred yards west of a temporary hut, not unlike those found on building sites, that serves as headquarters to Belfast City Airport Taxis. Outside, drivers tinker under bonnets, check the tread on their tyres, apply anti-freeze and bat their gloved hands together – killing time until the work truly begins at approximately eight o'clock, when the first of the airport's passenger planes arrive. 'There's not much else to do,' said driver Francis. 'We either sit inside and play cards, or walk around the yard to keep warm.'

Fifty-five taxi drivers – most of whom own and operate six or eight-seater taxi-buses, and all of whom have previous experience of working public and/or private-hire elsewhere in the city – are employed by Belfast City Airport Taxis.

'What you lift is what you earn,' explained one driver, Raymond, when asked how the setup worked. 'We pay an annual fee to the airport of roughly £250,000 between fifty odd drivers. Plus we're charged £1.50 every time we go through the barrier to collect a job. So we pay out roughly £100 a week.'

The 'barrier' that Raymond referred to is similar to any automatic car-park barrier, and prevents other public vehicles from entering the taxi rank in front of the terminal building. Fares queue up there and wait their turn, just like any other public-hire rank in Belfast.

Back in the common room, those drivers waiting for jobs can survey the rank by way of a CCTV feed, which shows up on a small black and white monitor in the corner.

'Taxiing is the same all over; it just depends on your

workload,' added Raymond. 'You come in. You sit. You wait. You get a job. You come back. Saturday and Sunday, you could sit around here for two, maybe three hours between jobs. A driver did a survey once, or whatever you want to call it. Out of a twelve-hour day at the airport, he only worked three hours. The other nine hours were spent just sitting around.

'That's why we need the office. If you have something to do, you go and do it. Otherwise you just hang about and talk. You have to have somewhere to sit, rather than outside in the motor. Constantly sitting out in the motor, you'd end up in hospital with all sorts of problems. Personally, I like to keep on my feet. Haven't had any problems myself, touch wood.'

With Belfast International Airport located sixteen miles west of the city, George Best Belfast City Airport, to the east, is the only airport located within Belfast's city limits. The owners of Shorts Brothers/Bombardier aircraft factory – formerly one of Belfast's biggest employers – built the original runway in 1937. They named it Sydenham Airport (because of the area of the city it was in); since then it has been called Belfast Harbour Airport and Belfast City Airport, until its name changed again in 2006 in honour of the city's greatest footballer, George Best, who is still much loved in Belfast and who died of liver failure in November 2005 after a long struggle with alcoholism.

Pat, a driver who has worked exclusively for Belfast City Airport Taxis since 1993, has observed how the airport taxi business has grown and developed over the years.

'There was a driver used to work here in a horse cab!' Pat divulged, incredulous. 'We have men in their seventies; men from all over the city – from Short Strand, from Castlereagh, the Falls and the Shankill. I'd say it's 60/40 Protestant and Catholic. It's completely mixed.

'Me, I've been working here eighteen years, through the good times and the bad, and when I first came here the airport was only a wee wooden box. It was all sheds, all along the old entrance to the south of the current terminal building. You could only get one car through at a time, so you had to stop to let other cars through. A Mexican standoff: who's going to reverse and let the other one by?

'Then they put a set of temporary lights in, and they knocked a couple of the sheds down so that two cars could get by at the same time, and made some cosmetic changes. Tidied everything up. Then, when they got the Birmingham and London flights as well as the Blackpool flights coming in, the airport got bigger and there were more taxis needed.'

Work was intermittent, however. Domestic airline travel was not as cheap as it would became during the 2000s, and drivers working at Belfast City Airport made do with the sporadic demand for taxis.

'Every now and then you might get a job out to Ballymena or Dungannon or somewhere like that,' confirmed Pat, 'but if there was a bit of trouble in the city, then people would get a taxi to the end of the motorway and have their folks collect them there, or at the Royal Hospital, or maybe out at the Sandyknowes roundabout, because they were scared of getting caught in the city ... but we looked after them; we didn't need sat-navs or books to tell us where to go. We were real taxi drivers. We had plenty of craic with people. But come seven o'clock at night that was it, there was no more work to be had.'

Ceasefires, the rise of affordable air travel, the regeneration of Belfast city centre and positive reviews from travel publications – not to mention the good work of the Northern Ireland Tourist Board – all came together to attract visitors to Belfast, and the airport expanded accordingly.

The low-cost regional airline Flybe established a base at the airport in 1993, and Ryanair followed suit in 2003. In 2001, the current terminal building was officially opened and, with business booming, Shorts Brothers sold the airport to Ferrovial, a Spanish holding company, for £35 million. Five years later, that deal was outdone when the airport was again sold, this time for a whopping £132.5 million, to the Eiser Infrastructure Fund.

'I've been working here twenty years,' added Raymond. 'And when I started, there were a lot less flights. But it's grown through the years. It's the same as anything; it's progress.'

Alas, however, the good times were not to last. While in 2010 George Best Belfast City Airport handled a record 2.7 million passengers, it was to prove a high point.

'Before, the cheaper flights brought more people in,' explained Raymond, when I spoke to him in 2011. 'There were no long-haul flights from Turkey or Spain, but people came here from the UK for weekend holidays, because the flights were cheap enough. We used to get a lot of stag parties and hen parties coming in, but not so much any more.

'I'd say we would be doing roughly half of what we were doing last year, because of the cutbacks, the recession, loss of flights, whatever you want to call it. We lost Ryanair, for example. Their destinations were taken over by Flybe and BMI, but they aren't charging the same as Ryanair – they would be on a higher price level – so a lot of people don't fly here any more.'

Traditionally, Raymond told me, it had been businessmen travelling to Belfast – to negotiate new deals or to scout out new premises – who had provided taxi drivers at the airport with the most work. But even those who can afford first-class air travel are beginning to tighten purse strings, and the fallout has been severe for those taxi drivers who formerly benefited from work from the regular business travellers.

'The vast majority of work that comes through here would be from the business community flying in in the mornings,' said Raymond. 'But from the middle of December right through Christmas, there's no business people travelling. It's the same in the summer months. You have July, August and September – our fortnight holidays, followed by the English and the Scottish. You have six weeks or more when there's nothing happening.

'Businessmen from Northern Ireland aren't using taxis like they used to. Because this place is so handy – we're not outside Belfast, we're close – they get their family to pick them up, or they have their own cars parked up in a car park nearby, or in their friends' houses. So work here drops like a stone.'

This is the general consensus amongst drivers at Belfast City Airport, and it would be difficult for any economist to reassure them that things are likely to change for the better in the short-term.

Robert Gardiner, another driver for City Airport Taxis who, during my visit, was manning the mobile phone through which outside jobs are booked, and which is passed from man to man on a weekly basis, agreed with Raymond's point.

'We have a three-man committee that makes decisions for the good and the welfare of the rank,' Robert explained, 'but there's nothing they can do about the recession. Ninety per cent of our work was all boys in suits. There were a lot of powerful English people came over. The Celtic Tiger and all that. But the gravy train has finished. It's sad but true.'

Some fares, however, do manage to make up for the general downturn.

'About a year ago I got a good job,' said Robert. 'Chinese guy, couldn't speak a word of English. He handed me his iPhone. Fella on the other side says, "Can you bring this guy down to a Chinese restaurant in Monaghan?" So I give the Chinese fella back his iPhone and away we go.

'Well we get down over the border, and I says to him, "Now you ring your friend." He showed me the iPhone – he had been sitting playing games on it the whole way down, and there wasn't a bar of power in it! So here's me away down south with a fella in the back who doesn't speak a word of English, and I have no idea where he's supposed to go!

'Anyway, we got to this town which was about the size of Donaghadee. I went into a Chinese takeaway. "Are you expecting this gentleman?" "No."

'We drove up the street, round the corner, and these two

Garda Síochána came out of the station, and here's me driving past, real slow, in a London cab. They just stopped in their tracks and stared at us. And I thought, "These boys are gonna ask this man for his documentation and I'm gonna go home with nothing!"

'It's happened before, many a time. Another fella drove a foreign national from the airport down to Limerick once. The guards took his fare into the station, took the driver into the station, and for a £300 job all he got was the £20 that was in this fella's pocket. Nothing he could do about it.

'But, thankfully, there on the corner was another Chinese restaurant. £212 on the meter. We left the guards behind, and these Chinese lads took me in, paid me, and fed me – table for one, everything! – and I went back up the road with £212. Job of a lifetime, that one was. Job of a lifetime …'

And this was not the only satisfactory experience that Robert had on the job. 'High-flying businessman left his iPhone in my cab,' he began. 'Well I contacted him, and you know what he did? He asked for my bank details and he said, "That phone is worth more than £250 to me. It has pictures and phone numbers and all sorts in it. So what I'm going to do is pay you £250 for your honesty, and wish you a very merry Christmas and a happy new year!"'

A lot of the drivers who work at George Best Belfast City Airport – like Francis, Pat, Raymond and Robert – have been part of the airport crew for many years. They know each other well, and the pack mentality that exists there – as it does in other private firms and public-hire ranks across Belfast – helps the long-term drivers to cope with the bad times, and enjoy the good.

Having experienced the heady days of the 2000s, when fuel was cheap, insurance low and demand for taxis at the airport steady and reliable, long-serving drivers are content to stick it out and find solace in the familiar, hoping that work picks up in the months and years ahead.

But what of those drivers who help to make up the numbers, the new recruits who stumble through the doors green, keen to wrap up the long-haul jobs and get the money rolling in? There are few newbies at Belfast City Airport Taxis these days, but fifty-something Jim Dickson is one of them. Having clocked up less than a year working at the airport – a very short time in comparison to the majority of his colleagues – he nonetheless had plenty of stories to tell. He explained that several other drivers had signed up then left in the short time that he had been employed there, having had their high hopes dashed once the realities of the job became apparent.

'After all,' he said, 'taxiing is no pot of gold. It takes hard work and patience, and it certainly isn't as easy as it looks. But I like it here, it suits me. Yes, there's lots of waiting around between flights, and long hours sometimes, but the guys are great and they let me come and go when I please.

'I came to taxiing at the airport in a roundabout way,' he continued. 'You see, I'm not the sort of guy who sits around doing nothing. I got hurt at work one time, before I came to taxiing, and while I wasn't well someone handed me an Irish history book, and away wee Jim went. I became a sponge!

'So I bought myself a taxi-bus and now I do a tour for most of the year, and, whenever the tourist season dies down, I morph from a tourist guide to a taxi driver until the cruise ships come back.'

Initially, after leaving his previous job, Jim found work as a private-hire driver with Value Cabs in the city centre. Things went smoothly at first, and then Jim had a brush with danger and decided that working at the airport was a safer option.

'One particular fare involved a lad I had seen in the *Sunday World*. He had been beating people up and had been told to get out of the Shankill. He was with four other people, and I soon realised that they were taking me to a derelict place to beat me up or rob me. As the journey went on, things just got more and more sinister. Thankfully, on the way to Stormont I saw the peelers. I pulled in, wound the window down and said to the cop, "I need these guys out of my car now". The peeler opens the door and this guy throws a crate of beer at him and runs away. £20 on the meter, and I'm out of pocket!

'After that I put an intercom and a camera in the vehicle and moved to the airport. If they mess around in the taxi now, everything is taped and recorded, and it all goes on to a 32G chip. It's a sealed box that I can't look at. I give it to the peelers and that's that.

'But the clientele is good here,' he explained. 'You don't get drunks. You don't get abuse, whereas, when you work in town at night, that can happen. And it's all nice, clean work at the airport. You very rarely have to clean your car. You might get a bit of paper or a mobile phone left on the back seat, but that's about it. This vehicle has to be specced [of a sufficiently high specification] for taking tourists; I'm here for clean work.

'Another fella who works for one of the private-hire firms in town was doing the 2011 MTV awards, and he was called out to a job. One of the celebrities and her entourage had gone for burgers. Would you believe it, she was sick in his cab on the Newtownards Road!

'Now honestly, famous or not, I wouldn't have treated her any different to anyone else in that circumstance. I would have bucked her straight out on the road! But this is the risk you take taxiing these sorts of people in town. They just don't know how to behave. I wouldn't take that kind of work, and that's why I work at the airport.'

During the winter months, Jim lines up alongside the fifty-four other drivers employed at the airport and waits his turn for work. It's clear that he is, like the majority of taxi drivers in Belfast, an amiable person, someone who enjoys and is adept at good conversation, and who likes to meet new people. The airport, with its regular influx of unfamiliar faces, and the unpredictability of where the work will take him, is the ideal place for someone like Jim to earn a living.

'For me, at least, it's probably the best stand in the whole of the city,' he confirmed. 'It's a lovely wee job. It's like roulette. Whenever you pull up to that door, you don't know who's getting in the car or where you're going. It could be a fare out to Holywood, but equally it could be Coleraine or Dublin. It's the turn of the wheel each time.

'And it's the standard of people you get in the cab: businessmen, people who are visiting for the first time, people working on films now in the Titanic Quarter. Usually I can talk away to people on a level, doesn't matter who they are or where they're from. "What do you do? You're a heart surgeon? That's great." I got a virologist in the other day. "Oh really," says I, "do you know about MI3?" And we had a wee discussion on that ... So you're learning about different subjects from people all the time, and, the way I see it, you're advertising the place at the same time. In a way, I'm an ambassador for Belfast – same as all taxi drivers in the city – and I tell people that we have a culture here.

'People are interested in this place, you know,' he added, proudly. 'The place where Milk of Magnesia was invented; where Titanic was built; where Jonathan Swift got his inspiration for Gulliver's Travels from exploring the Cave Hill. It goes on and on,' said Jim with a smile. 'That's the job.'

Driving as a Foreign National

> Belfast is a lovely city that offers everything at
> this moment. People don't feel it's a dangerous
> place anymore. I see many, many tourists in the
> city. You can have a very good life here.
>
> ALBOINO BIZZICCARI
> *public-hire taxi driver*

Emerging from the shadow cast by the Troubles, Northern
Ireland has become a beacon of hope and an example of hard-
fought but well-won and sincere political change. With the
pound strong and the European Union encouraging growth
and migration, Belfast is, perhaps, just the type of place to start
a new life.

Immigrants come to Belfast in droves and many find their
way to taxiing. In researching this book I met Russians,
Iranians, Poles – now the largest ethnic minority in Northern
Ireland – Americans, Indians, Pakistanis, Spaniards and others,
but some foreign drivers did not want to be interviewed
because they were operating without licences.

The two drivers I chose to structure this particular chapter
around, however, were both legitimate licensed drivers,
forthright and more than happy to talk about their personal
experiences of living, working and driving in Belfast.

Tibor Cervenak moved to the city from his native Czech

Republic in 2004 and worked for three years as a private driver, whilst Alboino Bizziccari, an Italian, finally settled in Belfast after some time in Dublin and Donegal, and continues to work as a public-hire driver.

Tibor was born in Hranice in the Czech Republic in 1977. A visit to the studio of Czech artist Mikolas Rutkovski sparked an interest in painting and, at the age of fourteen, Tibor held his first solo exhibition in a small independent gallery in Hranice. He continued his studies and held further exhibitions in Budapest, Paris, Venice and London, before getting married in 2001. His son, also Tibor, was born one year later.

With little income forthcoming from the sales of his paintings in the Czech Republic, however, and few jobs available in Hranice, Tibor began to look elsewhere for employment. But why Belfast? Why not London or Glasgow or Paris or Prague? Why not somewhere where the weather was better, the language similar and the history less troubled?

'I moved to Belfast by accident,' Tibor explained. 'There was an advertisement in my job centre in the Czech Republic, so I grabbed it and called the number. It was a leaflet from Belfast. It could have been from any European country or city where I could use my broken English. I could be going there. But it was from Belfast. I was one of the first to move from the Czech Republic to Belfast.'

Tibor adapted to Belfast well and, during his time working as a cleaner in Belfast, he never endured a single racist slur. 'Honestly, it did not happen even once.' He enjoyed his first couple of years in the city, and made several friends here.

As with all immigrants, however, it took some time for Tibor to settle into his new home city. 'For the first fifteen months I was living in a shared house with different people – I had one room for myself – and I worked at nights as a cleaner on the Dublin trains. I was understanding that this is part of life when you work abroad. You have to save money for your accommodation. You have to save money for your living, and you have to send money home to your family also. I had a wife and a boy at home. I was not crying, you know; I was excited. But now, when I look back, it was not that easy in the first months.'

Tibor continued to graft, finding work through an agency, and was placed as a cleaner with several companies in Belfast's city centre. He made a decent living, enough to send money home to his wife and child and maintain a relatively comfortable existence for himself. He kept his head down, worked hard and got to know Belfast. But tragic news from home soon brought Tibor's new life crashing down around him.

'At the time I was cleaning offices in the city centre – four night shifts and four afternoon shifts, full-time – and doing support work in a healthcare centre. My younger brother died very tragically, just one day before Christmas Eve. My mental health dropped down to a very bad depression. I was an absolutely different person. I tried to go to work, but it was not possible. My supervisors watched me more and more – they did not understand. I was in this work group, a trade union or something like that, but nobody helped me. Then my GP signed me on for sick pay for a whole year. I told my supervisors, and I was very surprised that they didn't support me. They kicked me out of work and gave me very bad references. For that reason I start to think of working for myself.'

In despair, and with little confidence that he would get on to the books of an employment agency in light of his bad references, Tibor considered his options. He continued to paint in his spare time, hopeful that one day he might be accepted into an exhibition or private gallery in Belfast, and, to make ends meet, took what he describes as the 'obvious choice': taxiing.

He did not much like the idea to begin with – he already had a UK driving licence, and had been driving in Belfast for two years, but there were many areas of Belfast that he was unfamiliar with, and he was acutely aware of the dangers

116

inherent in the job. But there were few alternatives.

'I taxi for the first time in 2006, and for three years after that. My first job was through Value Cabs. After that I was working with fonaCAB and after that, back with Value Cabs. Generally, I didn't have a problem with taxi work. I made more money than cleaning. But when I started taxiing I was working like a dog, driving all night and not going to sleep. I have to work six days a week, never working under ten hours, sometimes sixteen hours a day. I had just one day off.

'It was hard. The minimum rate per hour is like £8, not more. So if you work ten hours you have £100. It's nothing. But I have two children and a wife then. I need to make money.'

But working as a taxi driver meant that there were no 'supervisors' looking over his shoulder, and Tibor appreciated the help he was given by his new employers, who, he insists, 'were always good' with foreign drivers and those new to the job.

'The fonaCAB operators were very, very good, especially with me, because I was the most panicking driver probably,' he laughed. 'I was just a little bit stressed, because I had to find the way to pick up customer on the right time – if you're not doing that correctly you're losing job – so I am generally driving very fast – like I paint, very quickly. It's the same behaviour. But they were absolutely fantastic. They're not losing temper, they're not shouting. I was very delighted.'

Taxiing presented Tibor with its own particular set of pressures. He had no problems with fares and accepted the long working hours, but he found the geography of the city difficult. However, Tibor assumed a philosophical approach to his new work and looks back on those first few months as an essential and enjoyable learning experience.

'I always feel safe driving here. Generally I find Belfast people are very friendly. Sometimes you can have job, like a doorman, for example, he's working in the bar or nightclub and he knows, "Today I will have to slap somebody or fight." When I was driving I didn't have those thoughts. I was driving every day with the same behaviour and attitude behind my wheel: I was knowing how to behave. I was going to finish my hours and I was enjoying that, it was nice. And many times people surprised me with tips. I was very nicely surprised. I had an absolutely good time.

'But when I started to taxi it was a nightmare because I'm a very emotional person, I'm very nervous. It took me a while to find my way around Belfast. And for two months I was very, very stressed. I knew the city centre, but I remember once they sent me to some address on Royal Avenue – but Royal Avenue runs from City Hall to Yorkgate! I was looking for this address, but I couldn't find the number on the buildings. There were some businesses on the right-hand side, and there was traffic going around me, and I had to look for houses – and I nearly made a car accident!

'My friend says to me later, "Tibor, we were driving around you and here's you looking like a murderer!" But I'm happy thinking about that because that was a nice time, a very good experience. It was funny, you know. It makes me laugh.'

Thereafter, an uncertain Tibor turned to a sat-nav for help, but it was not all plain sailing. One ill-fated journey to Holywood – an affluent area on the eastern hills overlooking Belfast – ended in an unexpected diversion. 'In Holywood, I arrived at some street – I can't remember the name. There were flats, a cement fence and a tiny road. I thought it must be new, because it's not matching with the sat-nav. But I see this road, I drive in and I end up on the beach! I had to reverse. Sometimes, lots of crazy things with the sat-nav.'

Some months after Tibor started taxiing, he received a notice from dispatch to a familiar address: the healthcare centre where he had once worked. Despite the bad terms on which Tibor had parted company with the staff, he looks back on his time spent there as a happy one. He took the job without hesitation – and recalls it as one of the most memorable, remarkable journeys of his life.

'When I was working with fonaCAB they had an account with the healthcare centre, and I got a message from dispatch. "Number 13, patient from day centre. The patient is blind. She can't walk, she needs help." Because I was working with patients in the same place before, I was not averse to helping them. It was normal. Sometimes it just helps to give your hand and walk with them to the car.

'Also,' Tibor remembered, 'there was a return address that I was never driving to before. I was new to taxi; I was nervous to start. So I said to dispatch, "Before I go and pick up I should put that address in the sat-nav and check where it is."

'So I pick up this blind person and she say, "I have to sit in the front." I said, "Okay, no problem." I was driving to the Ravenhill area – I'm trying to concentrate – and she is saying, "No, no. Go to the right. You keep going to the left!" I said, "Hold on, I've got it in my data that you're blind!"

'She said that she's been driving every day by the same road and she sees the lights. She started directing me to her door – I was driving left and right – and she said, "Stop here." After that I sit in the car for like ten, fifteen minutes. I couldn't believe it.'

Tibor remembered only one assignment that he judged to be potentially perilous, and the warning signs were there: a dodgy address that he preferred not to mention and passengers with carrier bags full of beer.

When the inebriated fares asked him to stop at an off-licence, and left the doors open as they exited the vehicle, Tibor locked his doors, vacated the area and radioed into dispatch, who accepted his decision without question. 'I call directly to my dispatch office; "Excuse me, this last customer was very abusive and I decided not to continue with them." My depot respect that.'

As he became better acquainted with the various districts of Belfast, however – by then a confident driver who knew his way around the city – Tibor learned not to judge every book by its cover. He argues that certain areas of Belfast continue to be unfairly judged by both residents and visitors alike.

'When I worked in the city centre at night, I locked all my doors. Sometimes I see teenager with beer bottle in their hand, and I don't take these people in the car, because you never know what's happened. But you are the only person who can decide if the situation is safe for you. Nobody can decide that better than you. Always, I have these thoughts in my head: you are the only person who takes this risk.

'Once, at 4 a.m. in the morning, there were five guys in Donegall Pass. I was a little bit afraid to go there at night. Everyone knows the area; we have some bad feeling about streets like that. Lots of people speak about these streets and that made me worry. But I pick them up – they were speaking their own slang and they had fun.

'One of these guys was most strange. I had a good conversation with him about boxing and kickboxing. He was interested in that stuff. I finished the journey in the normal way and they paid me. They even give me tips. Actually, I was surprised myself.'

With his wife and children relocated to a semi-detached house in Belfast, Tibor finally gave up his short-lived life behind the wheel in 2009, three years after he had first ventured onto the city streets.

He is adamant that, once those initial months are over and the trepidation has been replaced by confidence, anyone can work as a taxi driver in Belfast. In other words, it's not as bad as it seems.

In the end, his art provided a way out of the dreary nine-to-five. 'I saved some money through the years when I was taxiing. I was not drinking, because I was out driving all the time. I was not going outside and I don't spend money for other things. I don't save too much, but I sold two paintings, and that was a really, really big help,' Tibor beamed. 'A good result. It was enough.'

★

Alboino Bizziccari came to Belfast for different reasons. He had no family to provide for, and no real financial incentive to leave Italy. But he had ambitions to make a career in the tourist industry abroad, and a curiosity about the island of Ireland. His family owned their own pizza establishment in Rome, and it was there – behind the counter, and out front, mingling with the customers – that he acquired a passion for different cultures. Outgoing and outspoken, he is, undoubtedly, a people person.

'I'm talking with the people all the time,' Alboino confirmed. 'Managing customer care. Tourism is in my blood, practically. I move in this business quite well. In Italy I worked as a bus driver for a massive Italian coach company. I cover national and international routes, all over Europe. But then I move from Rome to Dublin in April 2000. I spent six months in Dublin, but Dublin is London's daughter, you understand? It is too expensive. So, after six months, I move to Donegal.'

Alboino had learned of a tourism management course in Donegal organised, as he recalled it, by Fáilte Ireland, the Irish Tourist Board. Put off by the cost of living in the Irish capital, and fuelled by a desire to gain further qualifications, he packed his bags and headed north.

'I took a very general practical course in tourism skills,' he continued. 'I can do tourist guiding, ticket booking, reception work, things like that. Donegal is a beautiful place, but the jobs they have are very poor, maybe two or three days a week. So Belfast was the last move.'

Although Alboino is a proud Italian, he freely admits that he was left frustrated by the inept government, woeful infrastructure and nepotistic system that drive so many of his fellow Italians to seek work elsewhere in Europe. He was keen to strike out on his own, in a foreign country, and argues convincingly that Northern Ireland provides those with ambitions the ability to forge careers for themselves abroad, and gives them the best possible incentives to do so.

'In Italy we have environmental and political problems, unemployment, bad social housing. If you're not supported from your family, you have no chance to go on. In Ireland, you have the welfare system. If you're losing your job, they give you money. If you don't have any chance to be employed, they give you training. If you don't have any accommodation, they give you accommodation. In Italy, everything must be a problem. I don't like it. Forget it.'

Belfast offered Alboino a simpler life. Compared to Rome, it was smaller and more manageable. Compared to Dublin, it was cheaper and had a character of its own. And, in contrast to rural County Donegal, it was just the type of urban setting in which he might make use of his recent qualifications.

'Belfast is a lovely city that offers everything at this moment,' Alboino continued. 'It is a great city, absolutely. You don't have any trouble. You don't need a lot of things. The city becomes more international. People don't feel it's a dangerous place anymore. I see many, many tourists in the city. You can have a very good life here.'

When he first arrived in Belfast, Alboino found work as a coach driver, escorting tourists around Northern Ireland – north to the Antrim coast and the Giant's Causeway, south to the Mourne mountains and west to Derry and the lands beyond the River Bann. He may well have continued to work as a coach driver – a job that afforded him the opportunity to wax lyrical with passengers of all nationalities and hone his knowledge of Northern Irish geography, history and culture – had his employers not gone bust.

As a consequence, Alboino was left with no steady income and few savings to live off. Taxiing was a quick-fix solution, a stop-gap strategy on the way to bigger and better things. Already au fait with the rules of the road in Ireland, he took the PSV test, acquired his licence within weeks, and found work with a small private-hire company on Botanic Avenue.

'I start to work for City Cab, which is not there any more. It was a small company established a long time ago. For me it was an easy way to start, absolutely. There, the people don't complain too much.'

Alboino was pleasantly surprised at the ease and speed with which he was able to acquire his PSV licence. He compared the Northern Irish taxi industry favourably to those in Rome and London, and told me that the regulations imposed by Driver and Vehicle Licensing Northern Ireland (DVLNI) – the governmental body responsible for the issuing of PSV licenses – were not unnecessarily troublesome.

Whilst many indigenous taxi drivers view those regulations as too lenient – and, therefore, ultimately a threat to their incomes – Alboino believes that each city must regulate according to its specific needs.

'If you want to be a taxi driver over in London, you need to pass some test,' he explained. 'They want you to know everything: maps, customer care, safe driving, everything. But in London, taxiing is a different business. Just in the city centre, they have 26,000 cabs. My God! That means that the taxi is a very important public transport system in London. If you don't have any chance to go from here to there by metro, by underground or by bus, you take a taxi. It's an absolutely different point of view, a different approach. It's expensive, but it's still the best taxi system in the world.

'In Rome we have a small number of taxi drivers. For example, there are seven million people in Rome, more or less, that have come from all over the world, but we have just 7,500 taxis. So that means there are very few cabs. But if you want to be a taxi driver in Italy or in Rome you need to spend £200,000 to get a licence. For me, it's not possible. Forget it.

'In Italy, it's a jungle,' he remarked, 'because there are too many cars. People need to drive for their own business, so it's not very simple. But pedestrians don't feel that driving can be dangerous. They cross the road with people driving on like horses! You need to be looking everywhere, 360 degrees, front and back and left and right. This is very bad. So it's different in Belfast. Here it is absolutely fantastic.

'Belfast is small. It offers a reasonable time to go everywhere, so it's a very different taxi system. Therefore, you don't need specific knowledge to become a taxi driver here. There are something like 2,000 taxi drivers in Belfast, maybe more. Not that many.'

The expense of working in the private-hire sector however, eventually become too great, and Alboino could no longer afford to pay his weekly depot rent, as well as maintain and renew his car every fours years.

He also felt that, within the private-hire sector, some drivers were unfairly favoured by employers. According to Alboino, those with the most expensive and luxurious cars got the best jobs, so he was continually passed over for long-haul account jobs, not because of where he was from, but because his car was not up to scratch.

'When you're working in private-hire they can do what they want,' he insisted. 'I have never been in Dublin. I met a manager for a shipping company at the docks one time. His customers come from everywhere in the world. He tell me that he need drivers for Belfast International Airport and Dublin Airport all the time, but he met just the same five drivers.

'What this mean? This means that the company, they send the same people for the same job for the same customer. This is not fair, you understand? It's not fair because everybody working, everybody pay into the depot, everybody need the same opportunity. But not me? I don't think so.

'I understand that they don't want to send me because they prefer somebody else, and I don't have a super car. We have drivers in town that spend £35k for a Mercedes, they are favourite with the supervisors. They work VIP jobs. I don't.'

Disillusioned with private-hire, then, Alboino purchased a distinctive blue hackney cab and set himself up as a public-hire driver, waiting for work at the public-hire rank in front of the City Hall, where footfall is heavy and the demand for taxis fairly constant.

The public-hire sector also presented Alboino with a chance

to use his experience in tourism. Black cab drivers, whether official tour guides or not, can often put their knowledge of the city to good use by offering guided tours of Belfast to interested tourists. Many public taxi drivers welcome the added income that these tours provide.

It's pot luck if the next fare happens to be a tourist interested in observing the murals or any of the other landmarks for which Belfast has become famous, but occasionally Alboino is asked to drive to the hotspots, providing tourists with information that they might find difficult to obtain elsewhere. And whilst he is happy to drive up the Falls Road and explain the significance of the pro–Palestine mural at the corner of Northumberland Street, and double back down the Shankill Road to stop at a mural showing King William of Orange's horse rearing triumphantly, there are certain places in Belfast that Alboino will not visit, and will advise others against visiting.

'If, for example, you work as a taxi driver, you can help people with where they need to go, how they can get better transport, or maybe organise a little tour of the Falls and Shankill, something like that,' he commented. 'But sometimes tourists – Italians, Russians, people from all over the world – ask which bars and restaurants I can recommend, and that can be difficult.

'I don't recommend any strange sectarian bars or clubs that we have in Belfast. We have the same problem in Italy, so I can't complain. But you can't recommend these places, because if the tourists go there I believe they don't have any chance to come out, you know. This is true.

'There are sectarian people everywhere in the world, and they don't understand what they believe: who other people are, what they want, where they come from. They want just one thing: to live in their own house all year, then go to the same place without any questions. Forget it.'

Despite speaking out against the insular mindset of the sectarian minority, Alboino was at pains to express his gratitude to and respect for the people of Belfast as a community. For him they are welcoming and accommodating without fail, and the reason that he remains a driver today.

Alboino loves the interaction with the general public that his work provides, but he admits that the rigours of taxiing have begun to take their toll and that he still hopes one day to find permanent work within the tourist industry and leave taxiing behind him for good.

'A taxi driver needs to be working seven days a week,' he said. 'So there is no time for myself. Sure, I prefer to be on the road to make money, but it can be difficult. Sometimes you don't turn on the engine for two hours. You're still there, you know, but the customers don't come.

'It's not a social job. You only talk to people for ten minutes. Some people are very interesting, but you can't discover more, because, most of the time it's just picking up a person and dropping off.

'And we have hassles. The big problem, at the moment, is the diesel. Buying fuel now is a massive problem ... Diesel costs too much. How much time you spend before you get this money back? It's not easy.

'I believe that people who want to be something, they're looking forward. You are a taxi driver for an emergency job. For example, if you lost your job or you need a change, you can become a taxi driver for a while. But after a few years you need to move to something different. If I have any chance to move to a different job ... I don't know, to be honest. Maybe I become Italian president,' Alboino chuckled. 'Maybe.'

Day-to-day Graft

> Some of the stories you hear, you do honestly
> feel like a Dear Deirdre.
>
> RONNIE
> *former soldier and taxi driver*

Put a bunch of Belfast taxi drivers in a room together, lubricate proceedings with a barrel of beer or a bucket of tea, and they won't end up talking about bombs and bullets. Instead they talk about the people that they've met on their travels, the crazy stories they've heard down the years, the frustrations they have with the powers that be (in their case the Department of the Environment, which governs the taxi trade in Northern Ireland) and where they're going on their holidays.

Taxi drivers have acquired something of a bad reputation. They have a fondness for expletives, which can be off-putting to those who are not that way inclined. They enjoy the occasional joke that to some may seem base or offensive. Some less-than-scrupulous drivers – as anyone who has hailed a cab outside the Odyssey Arena on a Saturday night may be able to testify – are prone to either overcharging customers they observe to be veering on the wrong side of sober; or travelling the longest route possible – via every quarter of the city, it sometimes seems – before arriving at the destination.

127

And one young man who drove my fiancée and me to a restaurant on the Ormeau Road, where we planned to celebrate our two-year anniversary, had quite a knack for overtaking in residential areas, challenging affronted drivers to follow him to his destination – *our* destination – for a bust-up on the street if they had a problem with that, and laughing with psychotic abandon when his victims thought better of it and turned the other way. It is a profession that attracts all sorts.

As Billy Scott, a taxi tour guide proffered diplomatically, taxi drivers in Belfast represent a 'colourful mosaic' of humankind. They have their faults and they know it. Like all of us, however, the vast majority of drivers in the city share an appreciation of common courtesy and human interaction, and they have the tips to prove it.

So I wanted to wipe the slate clean and give drivers the opportunity to describe themselves and their profession in their own words.

'A lot of people would say that taxi drivers are just money-grabbing gits, that they make a fucking fortune and all they think about is money. But the majority are just ordinary decent people,' asserted sixty-year-old George, who has been taxiing in and around Belfast for almost thirty years.

George owns and operates a public-hire hackney cab with his wife Marilyn, and works the night shift while Marilyn works the day. Like so many cabbies in Belfast, George takes great pride in his work. For him taxiing is a vocation: a job to be enjoyed and not endured. It has many perks: the satisfied smile of a fare who may have learned something positive about Belfast during their brief journey, and the never-ending banter between drivers of all ages and backgrounds, some of whom have known each other since primary school, and others who have just acquired their PSV licence. For such newbies, veterans like George can always be relied upon to show them the ropes and welcome them to the fold with a well-timed putdown when they least expect it.

'You meet some lovely people in this job, and that's what

keeps you going,' he explained. 'It's not all about the money. For me, taxiing is about decency and respect.'

For Marilyn, her job satisfaction comes from the subtle rewards she derives from helping those passengers most in need. 'Because public–hire taxi-buses are now wheelchair accessible it can mean the difference between people getting out from one week to the next and maybe not getting out at all,' she explained. 'We help those people to have a life outside of their care homes.

'Take the likes of Roy, I've been taxiing him for three years now. He had a stroke. He's in a wheelchair and he's twenty-three stone. It'd kill you pushing him up and down the ramp into the cab every Friday. He goes to speech therapy. He can't speak, he just mumbles. But I can understand every word. No one else can. He'll not use anyone else, only me.'

As George intimated, being on good terms with people – forming a bond with customers – is something that some Belfast taxi drivers are innately skilled at. Deirdre Welsh, one of the longest-serving drivers at Value Cabs has been driving one old gent for many years, at his personal request.

'I picked him up at Central Station one day,' she explained. 'He had come up from Dublin and wanted to go to Portrush. Of course, I took him – it pays to go so far out of town. And on the way he told me all about his daughter, who had just gotten engaged, and about his family and his business and everything you can think of. When I dropped him off he asked for my name and thanked me for a lovely journey.

'Well, over the next few months he came up to the north a lot, and always asked for me personally to drive him to Portrush [a journey of about sixty miles]. He was a lovely wee man. We got to know each other quite well, and he even invited me to his daughter's wedding. I became close with his family, and I still am. But I will always call him Mr Doherty; I would never refer to him by his first name. It's important to keep that level of professionalism, no matter how well you come to know someone.'

Ronnie, another former taxi driver, believes that some members of the public come to rely on drivers because of their ability, if not always their willingness, to listen to their problems. The transient nature of the job – pick up here, drop off there – means that fares, safe in the knowledge that they are unlikely to meet this particular driver again, are often more likely to talk about pertinent, personal issues with drivers than they are with those closest to them. Being unaware of a customer's background, in turn, drivers are likely to proffer an honest, unbiased opinion on the subject. Ronnie puts this reciprocity down to what he describes as the 'Dear Deirdre' effect.

'Some of the stories you hear, you do honestly feel like a Dear Deirdre, and that's being truthful with you. I've had girls get into the car and tell me about their boyfriends. "What do you think I should do?" they ask. You hear about midlife crises. You get people from the gay community coming out and one thing and another.'

'I had a wee pensioner one weekend told me all about her love life,' adds Billy Scott. 'She must have been about eighty. She said she was a good girl when she was young and now that she sees what the bad girls are getting up to on the television she wishes she'd been one of them! She was telling me in great detail about going courting and this sort of stuff. You're talking about some wonderful characters. They either love you or they hate you,' he laughs.

So it seems that it's not courage or nerves of steel that you need to be a taxi driver in Belfast, traits that naive punters would have assumed were obligatory. For Ronnie, it's simple. 'You have to be pleasant and polite,' he stressed. 'I've been in some taxis and you try to talk to the driver and he doesn't want to know. It sickens me, it does. When you're in a job like this and you're meeting the public you have to be reliable and have a good sense of humour. To me that's what taxiing is all about.'

'There are very few guys out there who could really call

themselves taxi drivers,' private taxi driver Ciaran told me during an interview at the Taxi and PSV Magazine Show at the King's Hall. 'Some people don't like the job for a start – they only do it out of necessity. Well, if you don't like taxiing then why the hell are you doing it? That's what I'd like to know. If you want be a taxi driver, I'll give you the best tip of all: try to have a bit of personality.

'I was a butcher for sixteen years and I loved it because the people around me were always slaggin'. My father was a butcher and he said to me once, "Listen, see when you're on the counter and people are queued up, it's like a stage. Keep them occupied when they're waiting, because people get pissed off waiting. So you keep them occupied." And that's where I learned my trade. I love acrobatin', slaggin' people. I could talk to anybody about any subject in the world, and that really helps. Taxiing is made for some people, and I'm made for taxiing.'

'You have to have the confidence be able to deal with the public, so I guess it's not a job for everyone,' agreed Billy Scott, who is conspicuous at public-hire ranks in Belfast in his cherry red hackney cab. 'It does take a certain type of person to be a taxi driver in that respect. People react to their situations and their environment. If you're aggressive with the public then you should expect the public to be aggressive back to you. You're a public service, after all.'

So it's no surprise that many a driver answered my initial question as follows: 'What are we like, really? We are what the public make us.' Not every passenger is a prospective saint in their eyes, and it can be a subtle art deciding which fare to pick up and which to decline.

Overweight drivers told me of occasions when they had left their vehicles to chase after fraudulent 'runners', only to be taunted by them. 'Come on, you fat bastard. Keep up!'

Happily married men recalled instances when lonely older ladies would hitch up their skirts and offer to pay their fare in kind. After being politely dropped off before their stop, these same women would be seen waving down the next passing cab for another bite at the cherry.

Taxi driving is also not for the squeamish. 'Just before Christmas I took a boy up to Twinbook and I knew he was in a bad way,' recalled Ronnie. 'I said, "Mate, see if you're gonna be sick just tell me and I'll stop the car and you can open the door and be sick." Wishful thinking.

'This is the way he was – picture him sitting like this – being sick into his two hands. It was running down his shirt onto his chest and onto the carpet. There were wee bits of sick on the seat and here's me, "You fuckin' dickhead, I told you to tell me!" I had to get out and open the door because his hands were full of sick.

'You get the bokers in your car. You get the ones that shit themselves, pee themselves and don't tell you. If they turned round and told you, "Look, I had a wee accident there mate," show a bit of courtesy it wouldn't be so bad. But they don't, they just get out sneakily. These are people who either don't like themselves or they just don't like taxis.'

More worrying than a potential drunk or vomiting customer, however, is the constant threat of violence and hijacking that seems to plague Belfast's taxi drivers. Virtually every driver interviewed for this book had been the victim of an attempted robbery or carjacking. With memories of the Troubles and their murdered colleagues still fresh in their minds, it is perhaps not surprising that some drivers consider such 'minor incidents', as one driver put it, to be unfortunate but inevitable consequences of working in their profession.

'I was robbed one night in Poleglass,' George revealed. 'Four of them at 5.30 in the morning. They were going to cut my throat, and it affected me badly. I ended up having to see a psychiatric nurse to sort it all out.'

But taxi drivers are quick to point out that they are not special in that regard, that anyone working with the public is at risk.

'I remember talking to somebody a while back,' recalled

Billy Scott. 'They worked in a sweetie shop in quite an affluent part of the city and they told me they had been held up by gunmen three times in the past year. And they're working in a sweetie shop! So, any job where you're dealing with the public you run the risk of something happening.

'You're going to get yourself into situations and say to yourself afterwards, "Jesus, that was tight." But there are also very positive aspects of working the public. You can learn stuff, you can have good craic with them, and that can give you a great deal of satisfaction. Because 99 per cent of jobs are okay. If you're on good terms with people they're not going to threaten or take advantage of you.'

But while taxi drivers can enjoy the company of their passengers, they do not always enjoy the company of their fellow taxi drivers: the long-standing division that exists between public and private-hire drivers is still a source of friction.

'There's always been a conflict,' explained Billy. 'Because private-hire taxis, if someone waves them down they're going to stop and pick them up, aren't they? It's very frustrating for public-hire drivers. If you're in a public car, that's your work that's being lifted off the street. You get private-hire drivers who will blatantly pull up beside the taxi rank and try it in front of you. It causes friction all right.'

Billy remembers instances when private and public-hire drivers have even come to blows over the long-running dispute, which, he argues, is largely down to a perceived lack of enforcement by the DOE and the police.

'It was regular. It used to be on a Saturday it came to a head. As the private-hire drivers tried to pick up beside the rank, you'd surround their car, prevent them from moving, because actually it comes down to theft of business.

'But even if you approach the police, they aren't going to do anything about it, particularly on a Saturday night between the hours of 1 a.m. and 2.30 a.m. There are so many people on the streets wanting to get home that the police just want to get the town cleared. So they turn a blind eye. I'm disappointed, obviously, because it means a further decline in our business.'

Such disagreements between drivers are commonplace in Belfast, and the subject comes up on local talk radio on a regular basis. In the end, however, I suspect that private and public-hire drivers have more in common than they would perhaps like to admit.

In spite of the potential dangers of the job, and issues like rising fuel costs, bad driving, ill-behaved punters, insurance premiums and heavy traffic at weekends, like all transport workers, Belfast taxi drivers revel in the freedom that the open road provides, cherish the unpredictability of each working day, and welcome each new passenger. Most importantly, they like that they are their own bosses, free to come and go – to work or not to work – as they wish.

Taxiing in Modern Belfast

The world has moved on, and if we want to be
part of it we have to move along with it and
away from our own petty little squabbles.

BILLY SCOTT
registered Blue Badge taxi tour guide

From the 'chair-men' of the early nineteenth century to the
fearless hundreds who drove through the turmoil caused
by the Troubles, taxi drivers have always been in demand
in Belfast. But the advent of peace in Northern Ireland has
brought with it changes and new challenges for the city's
cabbies. It has restructured their industry, provided new
customers and shaped them, the drivers themselves – as well
as the private-hire company owners who employ them – into
better professionals.

The new Belfast is a city rediscovering its identity after
years of conflict. On one hand, the city is feeling the impact
of a severe global recession – new office blocks lie empty, and
many people are out of work. But on the other, it is enjoying a
rebirth – newly opened, multimillion pound visitor attractions
like Titanic Belfast and the MAC (Metropolitan Arts Centre)
have given residents of the city something to be proud of.

Now, Belfast's taxi drivers work in one of Europe's up-
and-coming cities, where peace walls may continue to divide,

but where the will to move forward is stronger than ever. Taxiing, in turn, has changed drastically.

'There are a lot of guys taxiing now who probably wouldn't have taxiied through the Troubles,' private-hire firm owner Trevor ventured. 'But, as the ceasefire goes on, the whole place has changed. From a security point of view, the checkpoints have all gone. Nowadays, you're not looking at people the way you would have looked at them previously when you think, "Where are you going to?" I suppose it's a different generation now. There's still the odd incident, but nothing compared to what it used to be. You're not as apprehensive as you might have been thirty years ago; you haven't that fear.

'The city has opened up again big style. There's a lot of investment, and you can see a big difference in the town. I remember businessmen in particular coming to Belfast in the 1980s – they came in the morning and they went back home again at night. Apart from the Europa, there were no other city centre hotels. Now I think there are about eight or nine, and they're building more. There are more people coming in – from the outskirts and surrounding areas – so the hotels are needed. And the more people that come in, the more need for taxis.'

Today there are many more taxi drivers working in Belfast than there were twenty years ago – there are currently around five thousand PSV licenses registered within the Greater Belfast area – but for the cabbies themselves, this is not always a great thing. With the increase in drivers comes more companies to compete with, more hackney cabs clogging up the ranks. And this is not the only downside to driving in a modern city. From a financial point of view, times are harder, drivers are forced to pay increasing costs just to stay on the roads – depot rent, annual PSV licence renewals, car insurance, fuel. Also, many private-hire drivers must find the added cash to purchase a new vehicle every four years, as many of the private-hire firms now dictate that they do.

On top of this comes the day-to-day risk of driving the public – carjackings occur, as they do in all major cities; runners will always be on the look out for an opportunity to bolt and leave drivers out of pocket; fares under the influence of alcohol or drugs will always be prone to violent or abusive behaviour; and the night shifts are no less lonely, the roads at peak times no less congested.

But there are many more feet on the ground and more fares to go around; and inventive, hard-working drivers will always find new ways to earn a crust in Belfast.

Individuals like Billy Scott have benefited from the new security and stability more than most. Now a fully-fledged taxi tour guide, Billy is an example of what graft and a little enterprise can achieve in the reborn capital city.

'You're still doing the bread-and-butter work, taking people in and out of town. But a lot of drivers today are diversifying, investing in themselves and investing in their communities, and you like to see people improving the profession,' said Billy. 'I'm doing a lot of tour guide work now as well, and I'm lucky to be in that position.'

Billy is one of only a handful of tour guides in Northern Ireland who have acquired the Blue Badge certification – the most prestigious tour-guiding qualification available in the UK, which is awarded by the Institute of Tourist Guiding. Perhaps, in years gone by, when tourists avoided Belfast, studying for the Blue Badge qualification might have seemed like a pointless endeavour, but with Belfast proving that it can compete on the global tourist circuit, the Blue Badge is now a coveted title amongst drivers private and public.

'I completed the Blue Badge course in 2006,' Billy added. 'It covers all aspects of life in the whole of the UK and Ireland – history, law, education, arts, literature, everything, because that's what people want to know about.

'It's probably the hardest course I've ever done in my life, but I just had an interest in how the world operates. You read up about it. If you get the opportunity, you take a course on it. Get the best people to teach you. And that's one good aspect of taxiing – between jobs, you can read, learn about the world. I think if you're going to offer your services as a tour guide, you need to know what you're talking about. I consider it to be a public service.'

Tour guiding is now a very big part of the taxi industry in Belfast. If you were to approach drivers at any of the city centre ranks and inquire about taxi tour services, for instance, chances are you will walk away with a wallet full of cards and numbers to choose from. Drivers who work for the likes of the West Belfast Taxi Association are now encouraged to learn about the history of the city in the event that fares pose questions about particular landmarks, murals or persons of interest, and the WBTA also run their own dedicated TaxiTrax tour guiding service.

Private-hire drivers too, who pick up tourists, are also more than willing to take a spin up the Falls and down the Shankill, or stop off at the new Titanic Belfast building – and make detours to places of interest, if asked to do so. It's a lucrative sideline for any taxi driver in Belfast, and most drivers welcome the chance to wax lyrical about the city for an added few pounds.

Not every taxi driver in Belfast wishes to be a tour guide, however. Many, while talkative and helpful when loitering at ranks, admit to being too shy, too uncomfortable at being the centre of attention. As well as that, Billy argues that some drivers who do profess to be qualified tour guides 'wouldn't know their arse from their elbow' – the gift of the gab gets them through. But even those drivers are making the most of the current situation; taxi tour guiding would not have been possible in the recent past.

'Up until 1998 Northern Ireland was a tourist wilderness,' Billy explained. 'Nobody came here. But, since they signed the peace agreement, people have started to come and visit, backpackers from Australia and New Zealand and what have you. Whereas before we would only have been dealing with local people, now we find ourselves dealing with internationals.

'I was talking to a couple from Australia recently, people in their sixties. I asked them, "Why did you come to Northern Ireland?" They said, "Our son came here as a backpacker ten years ago and he loved it. He told us, if we were ever in Europe, that we should come to Belfast." So from little acorns giant oaks are starting to grow.

'If you look at it, all we are is another state in the European Union, same as the Republic of Ireland, same as England, France and Germany. We're all part of one big community now. I think we have to realise that the world has moved on, and if we want to be part of it we have to move along with it and away from our own petty little squabbles.'

This new perspective has come about not just as a result of the peace process. The availability of information and the advent of cheap air travel are two reasons that people are beginning to focus on Belfast as a prospective holiday destination. The world is getting smaller, and Belfast is no longer a black spot. For the time being, at least, Belfast is a city less travelled, and therefore retains a mystery that all travellers seek. Belfast's cabbies are reaping the rewards.

'A few years back [in 2004] the United Nations voted Belfast the second safest city in the world after Tokyo; the safest city in Europe for tourists,' said Billy. 'Certainly I see that as positive. I like to see people coming to Belfast who maybe have a negative impression of the city – which obviously they've developed from the media through the years – and show them that it's a safe city now, give them the confidence to go out and explore.'

While the recent history of Belfast continues to fascinate tourists – and perhaps it always will – Billy contends that, with the 'opening up' of the city in recent years, visitors are keen to explore the historical minutiae, the little-known facts and figures that helped to put Belfast on the world map in the first place.

Billy is well aware of that hidden history. Erudite and

informed, he works his tours like a seasoned pro, but prefers to focus on the positives. After all, Belfast has many unique selling points on which to dwell – its history of exceptional engineering and invention; its grand architecture; its famous sons and daughters; its thriving culture and arts programmes; and the vibrant and pedestrian-friendly shopping districts. Taxi tour guides like Billy know that foreign fares are discerning – they want to experience all that Belfast has to offer.

'The majority of tourists are aware of the political conflict here in Northern Ireland,' Billy agreed. 'They want to be told how it happened. They want to visit the Shankill Road and the Falls Road, the most popular tour in the town, and you have to be able to tell them the history of the city, the origins of political conflict, how it occurred.

'In the 1990s all the press were interested in was conflict. Now they want you to take them out and show them around. And a lot of taxi tour guides would just do the likes of west Belfast, but I like to expand it out. Personally I don't want to concentrate or rely on the Troubles. I want to concentrate on how things have changed.

'Remember, you've got four quarters in Belfast: the Gaeltacht Quarter in west Belfast, the Titanic Quarter in the east, Queen's Quarter in the south and the Cathedral Quarter in the centre. There are a lot of nice art galleries and bars down there. It's so cool you have to wear an overcoat! And the big interest now is in the likes of the Titanic Quarter, the largest harbour development in Europe.

'People want to see where the *Titanic* was built. You've still got the drawing offices there, where the *Titanic* was originally designed. You've got Thompson's dry dock sitting alongside the Science Park – old industries and new industries running side by side. You take people down there and they get their photographs taken, posing like Leonardo DiCaprio and Kate Winslet. They see how Belfast has changed. Those tours are the future.'

And what of the future of the taxi industry itself? While

drivers welcome the influx of tourists, they are aware that the summer months are fleeting; for the remainder of the year they must rely on return business from regular users, but the taxi business has been hit hard by the recession. Belfast being a university town, many drivers have observed a marked downturn in the demand for taxis in the university and Holylands area in recent times, for example. They worry about the recession and the effect that it has had, and will continue to have, on their livelihoods.

With so many redundancies occurring in the public sector, and fewer jobs to be found elsewhere, the number of licensed PSV drivers in Belfast continues to increase, spreading the work thin and the money thinner. Combined with this is the threat of new legislation which will erase the distinction between public and private-hire taxis. From January 2013, private-hire cabs will be able to queue up for business at ranks throughout the city, and fares will be able to hail them on the street as they do black hacks.

But, whilst public-hire drivers are disturbed by such a fundamental shift, there are those within the taxi industry in Belfast, men like Stephen McCausland, director of Value Cabs, one of Belfast's largest private-hire fleets, who believe that such changes are necessary and inevitable.

'The new legislation will tighten everything up, and we're happy with the changes – the licensing of taxi companies; planning permission for new depots; staff and drivers registered with the Inland Revenue etcetera. In most cities throughout the world you can flag down any taxi, which is a sensible thing. The new legislation has allowed us to introduce receipt printers in all cars to prevent overcharging, and we're happy about that. If you open a business that involves contact with the public to such a degree as taxiing does, it should be licensed, controlled and enforced in the proper manner.'

Value Cabs has in the region of 600 self-employed drivers (the total fluctuates on a yearly basis) and 85 staff. Stephen inherited an 'addiction', as he calls it, to the taxi industry from his father, Harold McCausland, and his grandfather, William John McCausland, founder of Silver Cabs.

Over the years, Stephen, his brother Christopher and his cousin William McCausland – owner of fonaCAB, another of Belfast's large private-hire firms – have been demonised and vilified by private-hire drivers working for smaller firms, who believe that they are wilfully flooding the market with hundreds of cars in a bid to establish a monopoly over the industry. The McCauslands have also been criticised by public-hire drivers, who suggest that they would like nothing better than to do away with their competition entirely.

Yet several company owners and retired drivers interviewed – those who have experienced how the industry has changed over the years – admire and respect the McCauslands as innovators, shrewd businessmen who treat their employees fairly, seek to work with others and don't suffer fools gladly. They are the future of the taxi industry in Belfast, such people argue, and their example is something that all company owners – as well as self-employed public-hire drivers – can and should learn from.

It is true that the McCauslands have adopted aggressive business strategies in the past – buying out tens of smaller private-hire firms in all quarters of the city – but Stephen insists that he is now more concerned with the greater good, the welfare of his customers, employees and drivers being paramount.

'Yes, I'm very black and white. If something's not right, I'll let you know it's not right. But the taxi industry is a hard-nosed business; it's not softly-softly. And it's certainly not a business for an introvert. We have 685 families who rely on us running our business properly. And if we don't run our business properly, they have no jobs and people will have problems.

Stephen believes that there is much that can be done to strengthen and streamline the industry, to make it safer, more efficient and cost-effective for customers and company owners in the future.

'There is much that needs changed, yes. For instance, Belfast is the only city in the UK and Ireland, I believe, where there is no age restriction on the vehicles that are used as taxis,' he continued. 'The likes of Liverpool, Edinburgh, Glasgow and London, whenever their hackney cars pass ten years, they're worthless. They're in such bad condition, there's nowhere they can go – except Belfast.

'Guys buy these cars for £500, give them a lick of paint, straighten them up a wee bit. Then they rent them out for between £100 and £150 a week and tell the poor guys they have insurance, but they don't. They're a danger to the public. We want to have a ten-year maximum age restriction across the board, whether it be private or public-hire.

'About a month ago, on a Saturday night, the police and the DOE cut off both ends of Glengall Street to carry out an inspection of eight public-hire taxis. Two of the drivers got out, ran away and left their vehicles sitting,' he said, incredulous. 'The vehicles couldn't be traced to anybody. I would say they were scrappers bought from England. The chassis numbers didn't match, the licence numbers didn't match … I feel sorry for the enforcement team at the DOE, because they do try, but they have no teeth at the moment. There's no traceability. It's atrocious.'

During a meeting with the DOE, I learned a little about their undercover activities in Belfast. DOE agents regularly patrol the streets of inner-city Belfast at peak times – Friday and Saturday nights in particular – attempting sting operations to catch such pirates in action, or to try to prevent private-hire drivers illegally loitering for business.

But with so many hundreds of taxis on the streets at these peak times – all with licence plates properly displayed, whether lawfully attained or otherwise – it is clear that the DOE and the police have their work cut out. Stephen understands the difficult task that they face, but he believes that stricter controls are necessary.

'I was at a meeting with the police in Belfast about two

years ago because the piracy problem is just ongoing. They admitted that what the pirates are doing is totally illegal. "But," they said, "they're just trying to earn a living." "Well," I said, "so is a burglar, but it's still breaking the law."

Whatever a certain section of the sector says or thinks about Stephen McCausland, his professionalism is impressive – as is his office, from where he manages the day-to-day runnings of his massive fleet. The Value Cabs HQ is all plush carpets, original artwork and polished glass partitions. It's a far cry from the humble beginnings of Silver Cabs, and Stephen recalls the influence of his charismatic grandfather with pride.

'I didn't know him that well; he died when I was sixteen,' he recalled. 'But I did see him a lot when he had retired, during my early teens, and talked to him about his experiences. He still had a lot to give. I remember he used to come down to the Grosvenor Road office every day, and my father and my uncle would go with him for a coffee to a nearby café. I remember as a child sitting there in a wee booth listening to him talk about the business and it was almost like you were being allowed into this inner sanctum.

'Later, my own personal want was to go into something which was a bit more stable and quiet and easy – a high-class jewellery business, maybe. Open the door at 9 a.m. for five or six clients, show them my lovely products, turn the key in the door at 5 p.m., go home and have a nice life. I looked into it, did a business model. Instead, I've got 685 people to worry about and 110,000 passengers each week,' he laughed, evidently not in the least bit disappointed with his decision. 'I love the taxi business. It is addictive. I personally see every complaint that comes into this company, every day, 24/7. Because we've got very high standards; we expect a lot for our customers.'

For Stephen, standards are key. Belfast is no longer a stop-gap city for visiting businessmen, he argues. Nowadays they hang around, keen to see what the city has to offer, and invariably they use taxis to move between boardrooms and bars. Tourists are no different – every fare is important, every customer another pound in the bank. First impressions, therefore, mean everything, and Stephen believes that high standards must be maintained at all times.

'Our drivers operate within twenty guidelines,' said Stephen. 'Cars must be clean and maintained; drivers must have a good attitude towards customers; we have a specific royal blue uniform; drivers must not play the radio loudly; cars must have their roof signs lit at night so that they're identifiable, and so on. Our drivers are screened through AccessNI [the criminal history disclosure service], they have free training, and drivers of wheelchair-accessible cars go through a specialised disability access course. All these things maintain the standards of the business.

'Value Cabs is the biggest privately owned taxi company in the UK and Ireland. Any others that are bigger are co-operatives, shareholds by the drivers, and our example has been used many times by companies in different parts of the world.'

That example is evidently something that Stephen is very proud of, but he is not the only company owner with standards. Increasingly, smaller companies in Belfast are adopting his strategies, introducing uniforms, for example, and guidelines that all drivers must adhere to. Where the McCauslands lead, others follow.

From Stephen McCausland's point of view, however, there will always be room for improvement. 'We were the first company in Ireland to have a full GPS [Global Positioning System] computerised system,' he added. 'So when someone phones for a taxi it's entered on our system, and as soon as our operator taking the call presses the end key it goes to the computer for dispatch. The computer looks at the vehicles in the area and the GPS can identify which is the closest car within thirty feet of the job. And there's a new GPS system coming out next year that should identify cars within one metre. That is progress.'

Certainly there remain challenges ahead for Belfast's cabbies, be they private-hire, public-hire or pirates. There are differences yet to be sorted out and interests to be lobbied. But one thing that everyone who works in the taxi industry in Belfast is agreed upon is that a return to violence – the conflict and divisions of old – will never be welcomed by the trade.

'I would hate to see it,' said Ronnie. 'I've three kids and I wouldn't like them to go through what I went through and see what I've seen. People are happy now.'

For now, Belfast's taxi drivers are happy to be employed, happy that the streets are relatively safe at night, happy that the industry is changing for the better and that the past is in the past. My hope is that this book gives an indication of how far Belfast, and the taxi industry, has come since the ceasefires. Now Belfast's taxi drivers are confident in themselves, in their city, in their future. They look back only in their rear-view mirrors.

Acknowledgements

There are many people who helped with the writing of this book, not least my editor at Blackstaff Press, Michelle Griffin, who added and subtracted, chiselled and sculpted my original manuscript into something worth reading. It has been enlightening. It was also a pleasure to work with all those at Blackstaff who had a hand in this book, namely publicists Sarah Bowers and Stuart Quate, and managing editor, Patsy Horton.

I would also like to thank Oran Kane for providing the original artwork which inspired the cover design, and designer Wendy Dunbar for adding to the concept.

I would not have secured a publishing deal were it not for the hard work of my agent, Paul Feldstein of the Feldstein Agency.

By the time I got around to writing the book I had a number of well-connected drivers on speed dial, people like Jim Neeson, former general manager of the West Belfast Taxi Association, Stephen McCausland, director of the mighty private taxi firm Value Cabs, and taxi tour guide Billy Scott, amongst others. No matter what topic I wanted to investigate at any given time, they were always on hand to discuss it or suggest someone who could. I remain eternally grateful for their assistance and guidance throughout. I would also like to thank all of the drivers and company owners and managers who found the time to be interviewed.

The staff at the Public Records Office of Northern Ireland (PRONI) were helpful in locating the most unlikely of source materials. The staff at the Linen Hall Library – particularly Ross Moore, who works in the library's extensive Irish Section, and my wife Mairead Henry, who works there as assistant librarian – also provided me with documents and texts that proved invaluable during the research period.

A special mention must go to journalist and broadcaster, Darragh MacIntyre, who encouraged me to pursue the idea when I was a runner working at the BBC, and whose book *Conversations: Snapshots of Modern Irish Life* was always a source of inspiration.

Finally, thanks to my parents for their unwavering support, and to my wife, Mairead, who was always on hand to provide guidance and encouragement when I needed it most. I hope you are all as proud of this book as I am of you.

I would not have been able to pursue the original idea without the assistance of the Arts Council of Northern Ireland's Individual Artist Award, which I received in 2009.